PRIMERS

Drawing and Reinventing Landscape

WILEY

AD

PRIMERS

Drawing and Reinventing Landscape

DIANA BALMORI

WILEY

ISBN 978-1-119-96702-6 (paperback)
ISBN 978-1-118-54117-3 (ebk)
ISBN 978-1-118-54118-0 (ebk)
ISBN 978-1-118-54119-7 (ebk)
ISBN 978-1-118-83057-4 (ebk)

Executive Commissioning Editor: Helen Castle
Project Editor: Miriam Murphy
Assistant Editor: Calver Lezama

Cover design, page design and layouts by Karen Willcox, www.karenwillcox.com
Printed in Italy by Printer Trento Srl
Front and back cover drawings © Balmori Associates

… Their elegant necks angled down as everything sloped
toward the river more than a mile across there,
full of sandbars whose shapes
the water slowly rearranged, so no map
ever stayed exact.

—   Debra Nystrom
(from 'Pronghorn', *The New Yorker*, 13 May 2013, p 37)

Acknowledgements

Many scholars and researchers have helped to put this book together and have shepherded it through the convoluted two-year path of its writing, in the face of many demands that the design work in a landscape office demands. It has been a pleasurable experience, however, and I was helped in this by my editor Helen Castle who understood and gave me some breathing room when I had to extend a deadline, and gave support to my request for a 'landscape' rather than a 'portrait' format for this book, the books on architectural representation published as part of this series being all vertical.

Michel Conan, former Director of Garden and Landscape Studies at Dumbarton Oaks, was a careful and important critic throughout the development of this manuscript. In particular I am most grateful for his insights about my own work, and for always making me go further in the expression of ideas.

Lauren Jacobi – at the start of this writing, a graduate student in Art History at the NYU Institute of Fine Arts, now starting as new faculty in Architectural History at MIT – was a critical help in finding material that I needed as well as writing to different scholars to amplify particular points, or to add new interpretations based on new research.

Noémie Lafaurie-Debany, Principal in Balmori Associates, cast her meticulous eye over the whole text and illustrations and was a most thorough critic as well as contributor in seeing the lack of some things in the text, and excessive material on others.

Elizabeth Segal has been the excellent editor to whom I always turn to force clarity out of my prose, the quality I prize more than any other. She is always my sounding board and ultimate recourse to get where I want to be.

Isabelle Desfoux, a designer in my office, helped to try out different scenarios for our design for the cover which went through many iterations and different approaches in colour, theme and composition.

Finally, Caroline Ellerby was most helpful and patient in seeking the permissions for the many illustrations, but most of all in being tenacious when we were sent alternatives of images which differed from the ones we wanted, pursuing by hook or by crook the right ones, making for a better book.

Contents

Foreword

Attuning the Mind to the Ebbs and Flows of Nature

This is a challenging book for all of us who have ears and hear not. Changes happening before our eyes, even radical changes, may be obvious and yet invisible because they are outside the frames of our understanding. Diana Balmori makes three claims: first, that our views of nature are undergoing a radical change; second, that as a result, landscape architecture is called upon to reinvent itself; and third, that drawing will be a key instrument in that reinvention. At first sight, we may dismiss outright the radicalism of these changes. Everybody, or at least every landscape architect in the Western world, knows that a global ecological awareness is transforming humans' attitudes towards nature. After all, isn't it an ongoing process that started about half a century ago, with Earth Day symbolising that shift? How could this be a radical change now? In truth, landscape architecture took a radical turn with Ian McHarg's *Design with Nature*, which was published in 1969 – again, more than four decades ago.[1] Last, and most paradoxical, is the idea that hand-drawing could be a source of professional renewal for landscape architecture when computer screens have made tracing paper obsolete, and social media are about to displace the newspaper. These are the real changes that everybody can see, and there is nothing fundamentally new happening before our eyes. Or is there?

Balmori herself was involved throughout the last third of the 20th century in American landscape architecture's shift towards ecological and environmental awareness. She was also engaged in dialogue with her colleagues at Yale and in New

York City, who participated in the transformation of ecological thinking in science, in the debates it triggered in urban planning, and in its impact upon the arts. In her eyes, it is not the idea of nature as a living system that includes human beings that is new; it is the necessity to renounce a long-held and cherished belief in nature's capacity for self-regulation – that is, in its ability to return to its former state of balance after disruptions that have accumulated since the beginning of the industrial revolution. Nature is no longer a point of reference, a polar star towards which humans can try to steer the course of living beings, the climate and the oceans. Nature is an unfathomed becoming; and scientists, like oarsmen rowing a scull to a future to which their back is turned.

In 1638 Jacques Boyceau de la Barauderie, in a posthumously published book, recommended that before creating a garden in front of his mansion, a country lord should display the plan for the garden in the entrance hall, and then (hiding like Apelles) listen to the comments and criticisms of his guests before honing his design to perfection.[2] No more. We can no longer plan or shape the earth, cities, rivers or forests like a well-ordered orchard or kitchen or pleasure garden for generations to come. Establishing tomorrow's landscapes demands a new level of understanding of nature, focused on mutability rather than on equilibrium. We have to become aware of the forms of the changes themselves – the dynamics of floods and droughts; the courses of twisters, hurricanes, ocean currents, *niños* and *niñas*; the transformation of river beds and sea shores; and the paths towards survival of animal and plant species. It is a good time to open our understanding to what is before our eyes and draw some serious conclusions.

Landscape architects of the environmental movement under Franklin D Roosevelt concerned themselves with land erosion, river valley restoration and parkland conservation. More than three decades later, after McHarg, the focus turned to ecological restoration and to illustrating environmentalist ideas in corporate campuses and residential projects. Now we are confronting new issues. Today, cities and megalopolises are at stake. Their development is a major concern. However, city planning is mired in legal, economic and political regulations and constraints which have been developed over the last one and a half centuries, in order to build a fixed world, something like the Broadacre City proposed by Frank Lloyd Wright.[3] It was a poignant utopia. It took the freedom of the Usonian family as its central concern and sought to carve a place for each home in the loose context of an everlasting nature. We can no longer relish this dream nor that of any other utopia. We have to place the dynamics of nature at the centre of our concerns in the tentative reformatting of cities and city life. This is a huge task to which landscape architecture should make a new contribution. But how?

To answer this question, Balmori takes a twofold approach. On the one hand, she looks at the long-range history of the development of landscape architecture and unravels the importance of its relationship to the arts, and in particular to theatre, painting and draughtsmanship. On the other hand, she turns her investigation towards contemporary landscape architects trying to break away from mainstream professional attitudes. Both of her inquiries are deeply encouraging. Artists are responding to some of the same issues that concern landscape architects, inviting a renewal of historical dialogues. In addition, there are myriad non-conventional approaches by landscape architects who share a sense of responsibility to the general public beyond their immediate concerns for their clients.

The diversity of their design perspectives may baffle readers who hoped for new guidelines to emerge from these landscape architects' confrontation with the reality of constant change in nature or for the discovery of a new avant-garde ushering in a bright future for the profession. Balmori's inquiry points to something far more meaningful than the promise of a new style or a new urbanism. She looks into the relationships between three non-linear processes: working, seeing and nature. Nature itself is a complex set of random processes, some highly predictable, others catastrophic, with which of all us, including landscape architects, have to come to terms, whether looking at or working with nature. Building upon her own experience, she explains how drawing constitutes a way of engaging the eye and the mind in an exploration of the natural world and of disentangling oneself from sophisticated and misleading habits of thought. She explains how drawing may open the draughtsman to a greater awareness of changes – both fleeting and awe-inspiring – in the environment. She also demonstrates how different contemporary landscape architects have been able to transform these experiences into a great variety of projects, triggering new public responses to nature.

Balmori's pleas for a renewed attention to contemporary arts – inspired by fascinating dialogues between landscape and painting in past centuries – and for the cultivation of personal draughtsmanship, are not born from a reactionary rejection of the computer as a design tool. On the contrary, she calls for the development both of new programs for hand-drawing directly on the computer screen and of new skills in using those programs. Tablets should make this as inspiring for creative interaction with the physical world as manufactured chemical colours and metal paint tubes were for open-air painting in the 19th century. But it is not important which tool – brush, Chinese ink pen, pencil, chalk on paper, or finger on a touch screen – is used, although the result will be different with each medium. It is the renewal of engagement with nature and of eye–hand–brain coordination which matters.

Drawing and Reinventing Landscape does not advocate using particular drawing techniques, or even styles. It calls for drawings as functional links between the processes of change in nature and of seeing on the one hand, and between the processes of seeing and of designing on the other. In both cases, drawing helps landscape architects to develop embodied skills as they interlace what they are imagining with their observing of nature. It will enable them to carry fresh and personal experiences of engagement with the world around them into a creative mode of proposing or inventing new city-landscapes that resonate with the flows and fluxes of nature. The present generation has developed new skills through daily interaction with computers. Draughting offers landscape architects a way towards attuning themselves to the rhythms and vagaries of natural processes. Inviting us to go beyond the looking glass of final renderings and construction drawings, *Drawing and Reinventing Landscape* opens the door to creative imagination for landscape design in an ever-shifting world.

Michel Conan
Williamsburg, 7 June 2013

References

1 Ian L McHarg, *Design with Nature*, John Wiley & Sons, Inc (New York), 1992.
2 Jacques Boyceau de la Barauderie, *Traité du iardinage selon les raisons de la nature et de l'art. Ensemble divers desseins de parterres, pelouzes, bosquets et autres ornements*, Michel Vanlochom (Paris), 1638.
3 Frank Lloyd Wright, *When Democracy Builds*, University of Chicago Press (Chicago), 1945.

Introduction

There could be a no more apt introduction to the subject of this book – the representation of landscape – than the thoughts and reflections of contemporary landscape practitioners and artists. Designers in my office selected the quotations. Each chose their quote based on their sense that it accurately described the present state of the discipline. The core theme of these quotations – the upheaval and complete break with the past in terms of representation – is the essence of this book. An immediate sense of the maelstrom in the discipline can be gained by this series of snapshots.

The French gardener, garden designer, botanist and entomologist **Gilles Clément**, has emphasised the flux in the landscape as its essential quality. He argues this is not possible to capture in a design drawing. Creator of the Moving Garden, a garden transformed by seasonal variations, self-sowing plants and unexpected events, he describes how 'The design of the garden, constantly changing, depends on who maintains it and is not the result of a plan drawn on a computer or a drawing board.'[1] (Javier González-Campaña)

Martin Rein-Cano, the landscape architect founder and principal of the Berlin-based firm TOPOTEK 1, stresses the discipline's artistic character: 'The tradition of landscape architecture is actually an art tradition, the garden is an interactive piece of art. Landscape architecture is a very traditional and conservative profession, and without art it would become plants and horticulture.'[2] (Noémie Lafaurie-Debany)

A revival of the making of a landscape is now taking place. English sculptor **Andy Goldsworthy's** work is based on landscape sites and materials, building everything directly on-site without plans. Yet

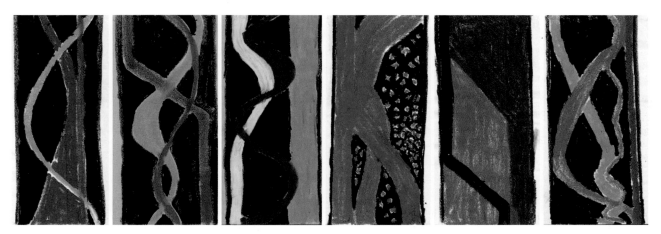

Diana Balmori, sketch for the High Line Park Competition, New York City, New York, USA, 2004. Oil crayon on paper.
Studies for paths for the linear park using color to differentiate various ways of moving through space.

drawing plays a very specific role in his work. In an interview Goldsworthy explains: 'There is a process of familiarization with [the] site through drawings that explore the location and the space. This is the only time I use drawing to work through ideas.'[3] (Mariko Tanaka)

Drawing as a way of capturing and developing ideas is explained by the late American landscape architect **Lawrence Halprin**: 'People "think" in different ways, and I find that I am most effective graphically and also that my thinking is influenced a great deal by my ability to get it down where I can look at it and think about it further.'[4] (Isabelle Desfoux)

Shunmyo Masuno, Zen priest and head priest of Kenko-ji Temple, president of Japan Landscape Consultants Ltd and garden designer, sees the act of creating a garden as the most critical moment of his ascetic practice. For him, the idea and the actual building comes through the mind and hands of its creator, not through drawings: 'A famous Zen saying is "when venomous snake drinks water, it becomes poison. When cow drinks water it becomes milk". This suggests that whether the garden becomes poison or milk is dependent on the creator.'[5] (Jingjin Zhong)

Noël van Dooren is a Dutch landscape architect based in Utrecht, the Netherlands, and also past chairman of the Landscape Architecture department at the Academy of Architecture in Amsterdam (2004–2009). He is interested above all in the representation of time: 'For me the starting point for research into innovative forms of representation for landscape is to take the issue of time into consideration. Film, dance, music, theatre, therefore have in common with landscape that they unfold in time. Think of the storyboard and the choreography of a dance. These disciplines work with notation forms in which the story unfolds over time and is recorded in a recognisable form for others. I am fascinated by the work of American landscape architect Lawrence Halprin, inspired by his wife, Anna, [a] choreographer. He investigated the possibility of the choreographer's score as a representation technique in landscape architecture. I see an interesting new way being created here.'[6] (Linda Joosten)

Anuradha Mathur and **Dilip da Cunha**, who both teach at the University of Pennsylvania, have focused their work on urban areas around rivers and coasts. As they write in their book *SOAK*: 'Our drawings often straddle the worlds of art and information communication; and they are indeed both. For us they are works of art and they are narratives, visual essays about the places we've researched. And though they are not always done with the intention of implementing the project, they do often construct the ground for projects.'[7] (Reva Meeks)

Bernard Lassus is a French kinetic artist who turned to landscape in the 1960s and in 2009 he was awarded the International Federation of Landscape Architects Sir Geoffrey Jellicoe Gold Medal. He rejects representation altogether: 'I had an exhibition in a space at the Coracle Gallery in London a few years ago. I hung strips of yellow paper from the ceiling of the gallery, suspended a plumb line next to a wall and put a level on the floor. I did this in order to destroy the notion that rooms are exact geometric forms. You see, people believe in geometric forms. And this is the big mistake in many present garden designs. They see a whole series of geometric drawings with angles, straight lines and so on, but in fact these don't actually mean anything. They're just drawings. I wanted my work ... to show that no room is completely vertical or horizontal. I enjoy such projects as they ask important questions. It's a matter of destroying misconceptions and examining what seems to be reality.'[8] (Theodore Hoerr)

Petra Blaisse founded the landscape, textiles and interiors office Inside Outside in Amsterdam in 1991. Her comments on **Yves Brunier**, the late French landscape architect who died the same year Inside Outside was founded, emphasise Brunier's ability to bring out sensations in his representations and how he tried to be predictive in what he showed: 'His plans described the future, they were predictions. They were not necessarily correct in substance, but in sensation, colour, light, feeling, atmosphere ... More than architecture, landscape architecture is a prediction. Whereas architecture describes a stable state, landscape architecture triggers literally endless scenarios of life and earth, rebirth, transformation, mutation. That's why buildings cannot live without it.'[9] (Noémie Lafaurie-Debany)

Frederick Law Olmsted, the American 19th-century landscape architect, creator of Central Park in New York City, wrote in 1882: 'What artist so noble as he, who, with far-reaching conception of beauty and designing-power, sketches the outlines, writes the colors, and directs the shadows, of a picture so great that Nature shall be employed upon it for generations, before the work he has arranged for her shall realize his intentions!'[10] (Mark Thomann)

This last statement, brought in as contrast, shows the changes from his time to ours. Olmsted expected nature to achieve over generations the landscape represented in the design. No contemporary practitioner would believe that today.

My own view is presented in different guises throughout the book. But as a point of departure for the text and a coda for my co-workers' collected statements, I will state that the changes in our knowledge of nature and in the ramifications of that knowledge in our culture have modified the discipline completely. The what and the how to be represented in landscape have changed so dramatically that I can say with conviction that a different discipline altogether is under discussion.

References

1 See Gilles Clément's website, <http://www.gillesclement.com/cat-mouvement-tit-Le-Jardin-en-Mouvement>.

2 In an interview with Martin Rein-Cano and Lorenz Dexler by Vernissage TV, 8 October 2010: <http://vernissage.tv/blog/2010/11/11/topotek-1-studio-visit-the-art-of-landscape-architecture/>.

3 In an interview with John Fowles, reprinted from 'Winter Harvest' in *Hand to Earth, Andy Goldsworthy Sculpture, 1976–1990,* Abrams (New York), 1993, p 162.

4 Lawrence Halprin, *Notebooks 1959–1971*, MIT Press (Cambridge, MA), 1972.

5 Shunmyo Masuno's website, <http://www.kenkohji.jp/s/english/philosophy_e.html>.

6 Translation of an interview with Noël van Dooren on the Academy of Architecture Amsterdam website, published on 16 December 2011: <http://www.ahk.nl/bouwkunst/actueel/nieuws/nieuwsarchief/bericht/voormalig-hoofd-landschapsarchitectuur-noel-van-dooren-promoveert-aan-de-universiteit-van-amsterdam/>.

7 In *Preparing Ground: An Interview with Anuradha Mathur and Dilip da Cunha*, conducted by Nicholas Pevzner and Sanjukta Sen and published by Places Journal Foundation in collaboration with the Design Observer Group, 29 June 2010: <http://places.designobserver.com/feature/preparing-ground-an-interview-with-anuradha-mathur-and-dilip-da-cunha/13858/>.

8 Udo Weilacher, *Between Landscape Architecture and Land Art*, Birkhäuser (Basel), 1996, p 111.

9 Petra Blaisse, in Michel Jacques (ed), *Yves Brunier: Landscape Architect / Paysagiste*, Arc en Rêve Centre d'Architecture / Birkhäuser (Basel), 1996, pp 20–21.

10 Frederick Law Olmsted, *The Spoils of the Park: With a Few Leaves from the Deep-laden Note-books of 'a Wholly Unpractical Man'*, self-published (Detroit), 1882.

The Contemporary Reinvention of Landscape Architecture and its Representation

1

We are witnessing a major break in the discipline of landscape architecture, stemming from a transformation in our understanding of nature. One of the characteristics of the contemporary view of nature is the acceptance that everything in it is constantly changing. This is the result of both the concept of evolution and that of emergence. While classical Darwinism assumed that all changes in living things take place gradually, Emergent evolutionists maintain that such events must be discontinuous. This shift in understanding means the end of most of the unacknowledged but deeply entrenched ways of working in landscape architecture and of representing landscape. For until recently, every design has had an implied end point, portrayed in a grand final rendering that harked back to a nostalgic paradise recovered in the design: a final, perfect image, fixed for all time. The scientific revolution of the 17th century viewed nature as rational and static – in fact, as the very foundation of the rationality to be pursued in organising human activities.

Beginning in the 19th century, a new understanding of a constantly changing nature slowly emerged. It was forged by people like Charles Darwin, who described the transformation of species over time (1859); Ernst Haeckel, the German marine biologist who first coined the term *ecology* and introduced the concept of an ecosystem in which humans and the rest of nature are bound together in a web of mutual interactions (1868); the French physiologist François Jacob, winner of the Nobel Prize in 1965, who saw human beings and the rest of the living world as a molecular bricolage in which old parts keep adapting to new functions; and the team of Herbert Bormann and Gene Likens (1974), who proved the existence of acid rain and the role of humans in creating this change in nature.[1] Over the course of a century, these discoveries and paradigm shifts produced a cumulative picture of a nature in constant transformation. They changed not only our understanding of the natural world, but – very importantly – also our understanding of the interactions between humans and all other creatures, between living and inanimate forces of nature. This is a direct concern of landscape architecture.

We have all believed that the sea would be the sea forever, the perfect image of everlasting existence. But in the late 19th century, scientists began to demonstrate how supposedly eternal and immutable things are changing. They discovered that various species have evolved and then become extinct, continents have moved and continue to shift, seas and oceans have disappeared, and even the poles have changed location, following seemingly haphazard trajectories. They thought that such transformations happened very slowly, that no generation would witness them within its lifetime. But recent events have led many to think that such changes are more pervasive and more rapid than was ever anticipated.

Up to the Second World War, scientists modelled nature as a fixed, open thermodynamic system with established laws leading to optimal states of the biosphere. Even after the emergence of the field of ecology, the idea of an ever-changing nature did not become part of public discourse until the 1970s – and even then at first only professionals began to see things differently. This profound cultural change is ongoing.

Origins

An examination of the origins of landscape architecture and the two dramatic breaks in its history may help us to understand the field today. In its inception in the 17th century, when landscape architecture was first recognised as an activity with its own specialised knowledge, it was woven into the arts; painting, above all, can be called the art that generated the designed landscape. Poetry, theatre, sculpture and architecture were also considered part and parcel of it.

The landscape painting school, in particular French painters Claude Lorrain (1600–1682) and Nicolas Poussin (1594–1665), presented landscape as something that had not been seen before the artist had looked upon it. WJT Mitchell has argued that landscape paintings produced the first unified picture of what before were separate unconnected objects, such as trees, rivers, roads, rocks and forests.[2] That way of looking at our surroundings, which came to be called landscape, gave birth to the discipline of landscape design. What the painters saw for the first time made it possible for the landscapers to design what they saw, following the rules of composition of a landscape painting – for example, using background, middle ground and foreground. Those who eventually became identified as landscape designers had often been trained as painters, for example André Le Nôtre (1613–1700). Le Nôtre, the creator of Louis XIV's gardens at Versailles, belongs to the first group of artists to be identified as landscape artists. The artistic view of the land dominated landscape painting until the early 20th century and landscape design well into the century.

Landscape progressed hand in hand with all the arts until the mid-19th century, when horticulture, botany, geology and scientific ideas began to take over the direction of the field, and its separation from the arts began. So total was this separation by the start of the 20th century, that when all the arts went through a major transformation together in 1911, landscape architecture was nowhere to be seen.[3] It did not go through that revolution at all, and for most of the 20th century it was a minor discipline supporting architectural needs. It was not taught at the famous Bauhaus in Germany, which had been created as a school where all the arts were united and that became an expression of Modernism.

Yet in the mid-20th century, in Sweden and the United States – two countries fighting adverse economic circumstances – landscape architecture demonstrated its ability to confront major urban problems. In Sweden, it defended the environment as a public good. The Stockholm School of Landscape Architecture played an important role in the transformation of the city of Stockholm and its environment under the Social Democratic government,

as in the case of Norr Mälarstrand linear park.[4] In the United States, it played a major role in the development of parkways that followed the boom in automobile production. The suburban parkways of Westchester County, New York State (1913–38) gave form to this new landscape. The Bronx River Parkway and the Taconic Parkway, both in New York State, and the Merritt Parkway in Connecticut, are good extant examples.[5] Landscape architecture also transformed a ruined river valley in Tennessee into a source of picturesque beauty and economic wealth.[6] However, this success was short-lived; after the Second World War, in the United States it resumed a mostly decorative role until it shifted towards the field of ecology in the last third of the 20th century.

Through Ian McHarg's book, *Design with Nature* (1969), landscape architecture made its mark as the earliest design profession to adopt an ecological perspective, and at times was even confused with ecology itself.[7] Simultaneously, landscape architecture also began to engage with urbanism, partly through McHarg's layered mapping analysis of cities and whole regions. In his drawings, McHarg gave an analysis of the different parts of a region which gave an overview of environmental concerns on a particular site.

These developments shed some light on the different associations that landscape design has had with different disciplines over time. In the 17th century,

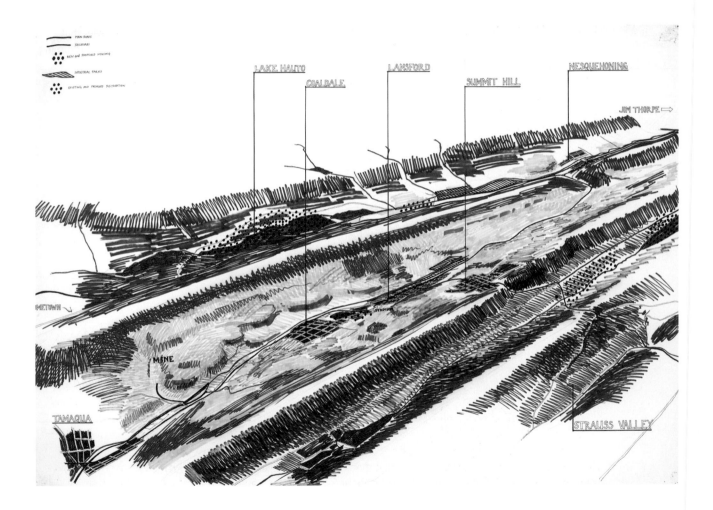

LAKE HAUTO

COALDALE

LANSFORD

SUMMIT HILL

NESQUEHONING

JIM THORPE ⇒

MAIN ROADS

RAILROADS

NEW and PROPOSED HOUSING

INDUSTRIAL PARKS

EXISTING and PROPOSED RECREATION

...METOWN

STADIUM

MINE

TAMAQUA

STRAUSS VALLEY

022

Ian McHarg, perspective study of the Delaware River Basin III, Ridge and Valley, Delaware, USA, 1968. Marker on paper.
McHarg's bird's-eye-view studies analyse the landscape at a large scale, using different parameters.

when landscape referred only to painting, the first terms used to differentiate the newly emerging field were landscape gardening and landscape design. By the late 19th century, it had become landscape architecture and was codified as such with the foundation of the American Society of Landscape Architects (ASLA) in 1899. Landscape ecology appeared in the 1980s, and now there is another reinterpretation of the discipline, with a new name, landscape urbanism. This history reveals the liminal character of the discipline, which allies itself with different fields at different times, taking on some of their perspectives and concerns but always continuing to exist as a distinct domain. It may now be time for the discipline to assume the word landscape by itself without any modifiers. It has ceased to mean painting, since you need to say landscape painting if that is what you mean, and it does not need to lean on any other discipline, though it does use in its work many different disciplines, but without any of them calling the tune.

Experiencing Change

Yet even in landscape ecology during the 1980s, nature was still considered static. One clear example of this is the concept of Clementsian succession, the idea of a stable path of a succession of species – for example, those of a forest – that climaxes in a biotic community in a state of equilibrium, where it then remains. *Design with Nature* and other works about

ecology that followed still represented a belief that while nature can be disturbed, it is capable of returning to a steady state. This idea has been supplanted by concepts of non-equilibrium, which show that most natural ecosystems experience changes at a rate that makes a climax community unattainable. The newer Gleasonian succession model incorporates a greater role for random factors and denies the existence of sharply bounded communities. Today, any professional who believes that it is possible for any work to reach a final state is met with scepticism. But there is still a resistance, even among landscape designers, to seeing all nature as being in a state of transition. Some continue to want landscape design to produce nostalgic images of some lost harmony.

Others, however, may find the reality of constant change to be awe-inspiring. Numerous time-lapse Google Earth images show us 40 years of winters making whole sections of the Earth white with snow; no year is ever exactly the same as the one before, in spite of the cyclical nature of the seasons. Through Google Earth we can also witness the rapid and dramatic diminution of Central Asia's Aral Sea over 40 years, half of it drying up completely. In this case we are seeing the effect of human agency as well, since diverting water from the Aral Sea to agricultural fields is the cause of this change to nature.

Landscape architects have responded in different ways to the understanding that nature is constantly changing, and have engaged in different issues of representation, as we shall see later in the book. Here, so the reader knows the point of view that informs my writing, I present my own response.

My first clear, conscious realisation of the role of change in my work occurred in 2005 during a project in St Louis on the Mississippi River. As I saw the river rising and falling, its level varying up to 40 feet (12 metres) in a year, and as I looked at a map that showed how the Mississippi had changed its course over hundreds of years, it began to seem absurd to try to contain such a mobile, ever-fluctuating element and fix it in place. At that time, I was reading John M Barry's book, *Rising Tide: The Great Mississippi Flood of 1927 and How It Changed America*.[8] He describes how two clearly opposing visions of managing the river emerged in the late 19th century. The builder of the Eads Bridge in St Louis advocated using reservoirs and outlets – spillways – while the eventual head of the newly formed Army Corps of Engineers wanted to build levees. The Army Corps won, and a levees-only policy was established.

Spending time on that river, experiencing its enormous and continuous fluctuations, and learning about its history,

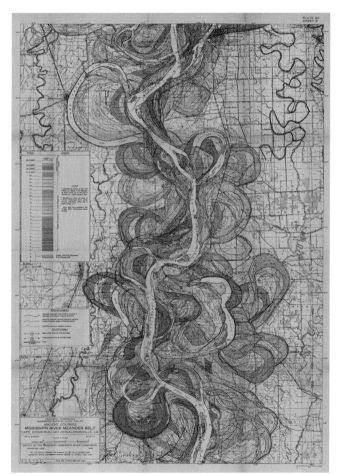

Ancient Courses of the Mississippi River meander belt, Office of the President, Mississippi River Commission, Vicksburg, Mississippi, USA, 1944. Print.
This drawing captures shifts in the Mississippi River's course since prehistoric times.

gave rise to a deep sense of discomfort which I had felt before but which I couldn't quite explain to myself. I saw that I was dealing with an extremely mobile, active, changing entity, and that there was a disconnect with the assumption that the way to treat it was to try to fix it in its course. By then, in every city with a river, there was a clear desire to have access to it. At the same time, it had also become evident that the typical treatment of rivers had been to send them through pipes, to direct them through channels, and to line them with railroads or highways, so that they became invisible or inaccessible to the surrounding population. Was there another way of treating them so that they could be seen and directly experienced? Now that we could view both rivers and ourselves as part of nature, was there another way of connecting to them and of accepting that they would be constantly changing?

I made several proposals for the project in St Louis. The public voted enthusiastically for the one that offered the greatest possibility of personal engagement with the river by allowing visitors to walk on floating islands and thus experience its many different aspects. With a very good naval architect, I then developed a system of islands that would be open to public use. They would rise and fall with the level of the water and could be closed off when the river became turbulent. The design would change along with the fluctuations of the river; the floating islands would be raised high at times, looking out above the shore, and sunken low at others, with only the edge of the shore visible from them.

This was a project to enable the citizens of St Louis to rediscover their long-standing relationship with the river, to perceive their lives as part of a unity comprised of the river and the city, and to reflect together on the changes that would take place over the coming years in this city-river environment. Developing a shared understanding of this dynamic unity is the challenge of the next several decades; landscape architecture has to find a way of helping people to meet that challenge. During the last 40 years, landscape architects have produced pleasurable landscapes as well as some remarkably didactic ones, but none of them has engendered a major shift in people's understanding of nature.

After working on the St Louis project and another one in Memphis, further down the Mississippi, I became extremely dissatisfied with how such projects were represented. Renderings prepared for public presentation highlight public activities and landscape furnishings set in the natural background, which communicates both a distance between people and nature and a sense of nature as a fixed entity. So, together with others in my office, I began to experiment with different ways of representing projects that instead embrace the reality that nature is constantly changing. I'll return to those attempts at the end of this book.

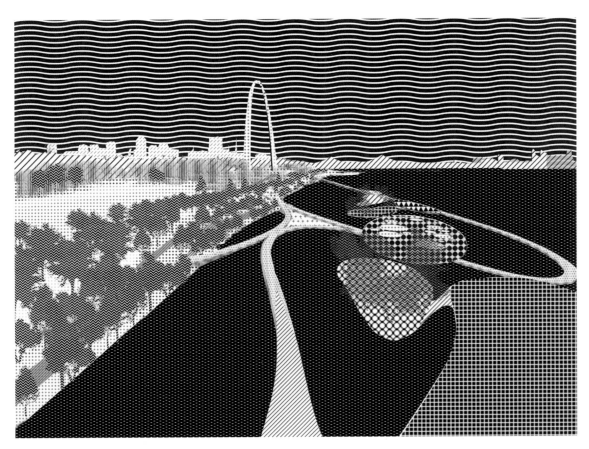

Balmori Associates, St Louis waterfront, St Louis, Missouri, USA, 2008. Digital rendering.
This proposed project in Missouri reconnects the city with the Mississippi River by creating floating islands that underscore the river's changeability.

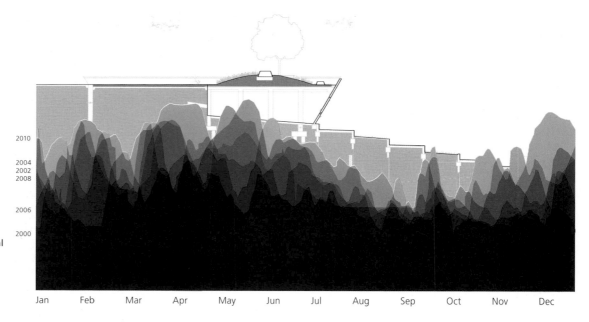

Balmori Associates, Beale Street Landing, Memphis, Tennessee, USA, 2011. Digital elevation and chart.
Varying colours represent recent vertical fluctuations in the Mississippi River.

Jan   Feb   Mar   Apr   May   Jun   Jul   Aug   Sep   Oct   Nov   Dec

Accepting the reality that change is the essence of all living things and of all designed and built landscapes presents many challenges. The experience I had when I was visiting a site in Mumbai for which I was doing a masterplan illustrates some of those issues; two projects in Seattle highlight yet others.

While I was in Mumbai in September 2010, a raging storm hit the area, and by all expectations the site – which was very close to the coast – should have been flooded. However, there was a very wide stand of mangroves between the sea and the site, and it was extraordinary to see their effect in diminishing the impact of the storm: the site was spared. So I suggested that the client try not only to preserve as many of the mangroves near the site as possible (the land was only partly theirs), but also to introduce new mangroves into the water storage and water purification areas of the site as part of its drainage system. Although the client considered mangroves to be weeds and rejected the idea at first, after lengthy discussions agreement was reached.

But this was a short-lived victory. Later, a colleague experienced another storm further up the coast. He was told by people living there that the mangroves were dying and that the multitude of fish species usually found in mangrove forests – which sustain some of the richest variety of biota in the world – had therefore also disappeared. The slow death of the mangroves was caused by the rise in the level of the ocean, which is a worldwide phenomenon. The

mangrove forest is a very sensitive system; the trees and the species that live among their roots can only survive in a certain depth of water. As a result, mangroves – so beneficial in protecting a coastline from storms and in supporting a rich variety of sea life, which in turn supports large human populations who depend on that marine life for their sustenance and as a source of income – are disappearing. In light of this, should we create floating islands that rise with the sea for mangrove forests to grow on?

For a flood control and water purification project near Seattle, Lorna Jordan constructed

Balmori Associates, Godrej masterplan, Mumbai, India, 2010. Digital diagram.
Here water trees act as above-ground artificial aquifers that adapt to water quantity available.

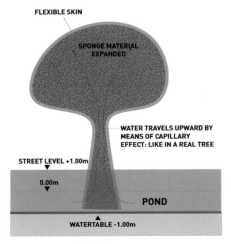

FLEXIBLE SKIN

SPONGE MATERIAL EXPANDED

WATER TRAVELS UPWARD BY MEANS OF CAPILLARY EFFECT: LIKE IN A REAL TREE

STREET LEVEL +1.00m

0.00m

POND

WATERTABLE -1.00m

Filled after monsoon

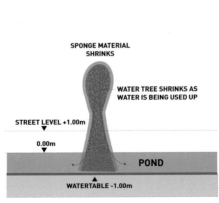

SPONGE MATERIAL SHRINKS

WATER TREE SHRINKS AS WATER IS BEING USED UP

STREET LEVEL +1.00m

0.00m

POND

WATERTABLE -1.00m

EMPTY - option 1 before monsoon

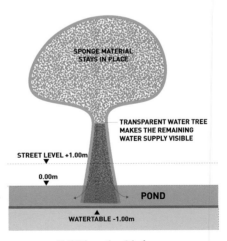

SPONGE MATERIAL STAYS IN PLACE

TRANSPARENT WATER TREE MAKES THE REMAINING WATER SUPPLY VISIBLE

STREET LEVEL +1.00m

0.00m

POND

WATERTABLE -1.00m

EMPTY - option 2 before monsoon

Herbert Bayer, Mill Creek Canyon Earthworks, Kent, Washington, USA, 1982. Photographic panorama. Bayer designed rolling hills and depressions to create recreational landforms while tackling flooding issues. This photograph was taken in 2008.

Waterworks Gardens (1990–96), a system of pools and marshes with different landscapes making a loop woven together by a designed path. Over time the system has been overrun by marsh plants. The original series of spaces along the path is completely gone now; only the red ceramic work remains there. Should this landscape have been restored to Jordan's original design? Should it have been preserved, unchanged, at some specific point? Should it be managed so that the only changes allowed are those that permit the various spaces to remain differentiated? These are the types of questions already confronting us.

In September 2012 when I visited Herbert Bayer's Mill Creek Canyon Earthworks (1982) in Kent, Washington, with my Yale School of Architecture students, I had a similar experience (Herbert Bayer's drawing for this project is illustrated in Chapter 3). Also located on the outskirts of Seattle, this famous project, one of the first landscape designs with an ecological

purpose – managing the water that was entering from the heavily built surrounding area and eroding the park – was shaped artistically and became, as originally designed, a successful public space.

I had seen the project 10 years earlier and was surprised by how much smaller it now looked. In addition, its edges were being taken over by forest, making the scheme and the spaces less readable, but the diminution was the most dramatic change. I spoke to Kent's cultural programmes manager, Cheryl Dos Remedios, who explained that the Corps of Engineers and the local branch of the Environmental Protection Agency had decided to build an earth wall that could withstand a 1,000-year storm at the site. Bayer had been charged with designing a system that would protect the park from flooding in a 100-year storm. I suddenly realised that it was this new colossal earth wall that made Bayer's structures seem so much smaller. Yet even as miniatures, they still did a much better job of damming floodwater, although they were diminished by the new intervention and made to appear insignificant alongside it. They were also still beautiful and still created a good public space, while the new earth wall did nothing but read as a structure that annihilated occupiable space. So the park has lost a true work of art and a successful public space, as well as the vision that the earlier town commission had for Kent.

The new standards for flood protection represent the kind of change we will now constantly be facing. The particular conundrum of Mill Creek Canyon Earthworks is not as difficult as some others. In this case, it is clear that what was needed was somebody of the artistic talent of Herbert Bayer to make the changes necessary to meet the new environmental conditions.

Breaking with the Past

Let me summarise the challenge for landscape architecture that underlies this book. The major transformation in the discipline that occurred in the 19th century, when landscape architecture broke away from all the arts, is now echoed by another break of equal importance and perhaps greater magnitude: the earlier concept of nature as a static, homogeneous entity that is entirely separate from the human race has given way to the understanding that nature is heterogeneous and constantly changing, and that we are an intrinsic part of it. New landscape architecture is engaged in educating the public and the client in the processes of nature. Creating representations of design projects that guide the imagination in that direction is an essential element of the process.

There are, of course, other important aspects of the current break in the discipline. Seeing ourselves as part of nature demands a different relationship to it, and the change of scale in landscape design projects, which can now encompass whole cities or regions, forces us to search for a different way of looking at landscape. But it is the acceptance of – and considerable vulnerability to – constant change which makes the discipline stand apart, giving it new significance in a world that remains attached to fixity and putting landscape architecture in the vanguard of dealing with contemporary conditions.

This has a profound impact on the forms of representation of landscape architecture. Because drawing is its main tool of expression, it will use drawing in trying, as landscape painting did in the 17th century, to present something that has never been seen before. We will see the new landscape only when we apply an artistic process such as drawing – whether by hand or by computer – to shape the way we see.

References

1 Charles Darwin, *On the Origin of Species by Means of Natural Selection, or the Preservation of Favoured Races in the Struggle for Life*, John Murray (London), 1859; Ernst Haeckel, *Natürliche Schöpfungsgeschichte*, Reimer (Berlin), 1868; F Herbert Bormann and Gene E Likens, 'Acid Rain: A Serious Regional Environmental Problem', *Science*, New Series, Vol 184, Issue 4142 (14 June 1974), pp 1176–79. Also see François Jacob, 'Le Bricolage de l'Évolution', *Le Jeu des Possibles*, Fayard (Paris), 1981, pp 70 and 86; and François Jacob and Jacques Monod,

'Genetic Regulatory Mechanisms in the Synthesis of Proteins', *Journal of Molecular Biology*, Vol 3, Issue 3 (1961), pp 318–56.
2 WJT Mitchell, *Landscape and Power*, University of Chicago Press (Chicago), 1994, pp 12–13.
3 Leah Dickerman and Matthew Affron, *Inventing Abstraction, 1910–1925: How a Radical Idea Changed Modern Art*, Museum of Modern Art (New York), 2012.
4 Thorbjörn Andersson, 'Swedish Mid-Century Utopia: Park Design as a Tool for Societal Improvements', in Michel Conan and Chen Whangheng (eds),

Gardens, City Life and Culture, Dumbarton Oaks (Washington, DC), 2008, pp 156–72, see pp 163 and 166.
5 Phoebe Cutler, *The Public Landscape of the New Deal*, Yale University Press (New Haven), 1985; Gregory T Cushman, 'Environmental Therapy for Soil and Social Erosion: Landscape Architecture and Depression-Era Highway Construction in Texas', in Michel Conan (ed), *Environmentalism in Landscape Architecture*, Dumbarton Oaks (Washington, DC), 2000, pp 45–70.

6 Brian Black, 'Organic Planning: Ecology and Design in the Landscape of the Tennessee Valley Authority, 1933–45', in Michel Conan (ed), *Environmentalism in Landscape Architecture*, Dumbarton Oaks (Washington, DC), 2000, pp 71–96.
7 Ian L McHarg, *Design with Nature*, John Wiley & Sons, Inc (New York), 1992.
8 John M Barry, *Rising Tide: The Great Mississippi Flood of 1927 and How It Changed America*, Simon & Schuster (New York), 1998.

2
The Pleasure of Drawing

It is hard to communicate the pleasure of drawing.

Acadia National Park, Maine, 11am, August 2012
The view of the sea from above pink granite cliffs in Acadia National Park in Maine is my subject today. I didn't know what I would draw when I sat down, but the surface of the sea is one of the most powerful visual magnets for me. At first glance, it's the colour that I find captivating. As I start to draw, its deep blue-green has changed to a duller and darker aquamarine. Do you stay with what first attracted you or go on to the transformed image before your eyes? Often you make that shift if the new image proves to be more enduring. And this one does, as a whitish veil of clouds takes away the intensity of colour.

In what order do the marks you draw go down on the blank sheet? What comes first? Here certainly the horizon line, the strongest line in the picture, the line between the sea and the sky. The island in the sea is uninteresting, although that too is a feature of the horizon. What is visually compelling is that at first this appeared to be a single surface of glorious brilliant colour. Yet looking at it in detail, the surface is crisscrossed by currents and so divided into varied pieces. It is alive with movement, with foam lines appearing where waves have crashed against the rocks, with smooth mirror-like bits and rougher pieces in many colours. The skyline – as sharp as a knife's edge when I started – begins to dissipate and becomes fuzzy with the gaseous white veil descending on it. How do you absorb this constant mobility of everything around you when you sit down and draw? It is an exercise in capturing a moment that is gone before you have begun to grasp it. A beautiful afternoon, if now a bit greyish.

Diana Balmori, 11am, August
2012, Acadia National Park,
Bar Harbor, Maine, USA.
Coloured pencil.
The sea is a constant subject of
exploration. Its surface, colour,
reflectivity and transparency
undergo continuous
transformations.

Nantucket, Massachusetts, 4pm, August, 2012

What is it about this nearly stormy day with patches of brilliant light allowing the sea to retain some colour? So animated and active, it breaks into small white waves here and there, with a sense of excitement about it, the breeze swallowed in gulps while you watch it. And as always in drawing, the light changes – the sea has become mercurial and quicksilver, now with a quality of zinc to its surface. That is precisely what stirred Le Nôtre when he created the vast surfaces of water reflecting the sky in Chantilly.[1] I didn't get it at first. The sea constantly catches these different moods and lights. I think the first time I saw Chantilly, it was a sunny cloudless day; if I remember correctly, it was around noon. It's better when there is more happening, and the light is more horizontal.

Of course, I am aware that I am excluding the front plane, the beach edge in Nantucket, avoiding dealing with what landscape representation worked so hard throughout history to resolve: how do you show a front plane together with a middle plane and a back plane? Centuries of effort went into solving that problem, and then the Modern Movement did away with it all. Or rather, in Modernism the background advanced to the foreground and took over the whole picture. What keeps this drawing from being Modern or Postmodern and enables it to hold on to Realism is the horizon line. If I were to eliminate it, the drawing would become Modern. But because of my own preoccupation with the horizon line, I begin with it when designing a landscape.

The Act of Drawing

By writing about the moment of drawing and the pleasure derived from it, I have been trying to bring attention to the act of drawing itself. This immediately raises the question of media. Is the pleasure the same if you draw with graphite pencil as if you use ink and brush? Is it the same if you are drawing with a computer?

There is no doubt that certain graphite leads (in my case, 6B pencils) and certain papers with a grainy surface, such as newsprint or an expensive heavy, rough paper, add to the pleasure of drawing. Similarly, the right brush – whether one that comes to a fine point, or one that can create a flat, thick line – and paper that is absorbent, but not excessively so, seem indispensable and add to the pleasure of painting in watercolour or ink.

And computer drawing? I want to make it clear immediately that I am referring only to the computer drawings made by working directly on the screen; they are the only ones that interest me, because they involve the physical act of drawing with your fingers. I hope eventually that will be possible with all computer drawing programs. Introduced as an app for the 2007 iPhone (eg Brushes), it has now new iterations for the 2010 iPad.

Diana Balmori, 4pm,
August 2012, Nantucket,
Massachusetts, USA.
Coloured pencil.
This drawing conveys the
movement and colour of light
on water.

Computing has been blamed for the end of the use of drawing and painting in renderings. But in fact, you can both draw and paint with the computer. It is curious that this modern medium re-establishes a connection between landscape and painting, for painting above all can be seen as the art that generated landscape design. In its inception in the 17th century, when it was first recognised as an activity with its own specialised knowledge, landscape design was woven into the arts. Poetry and theatre were also considered an integral part of it, as was sculpture and, to a certain degree, architecture.

Of course, computer painting is virtual. Or is it? True, there are no colours dissolved in water in these paintings; the materiality has disappeared. Programs in the form of apps, such as Brushes, are hybrids. They allow you to use your fingers to produce lines or brushstrokes of different thicknesses, textures and colours that feel as though they were created with a painter's array of tools. For example, you can achieve something like the transparency of washes of colour done with watercolour or the solidity and flowing character of paint on a surface. The English painter David Hockney, who is always interested in new technology has, since 2008, produced beautiful iPhone paintings using the Brushes app. He then followed in 2010 with drawings on the iPad, for which he has had a special pocket built into his jackets, following the architects' tradition of the inner pocket for a

David Hockney, *The Arrival of Spring in Woldgate, East Yorkshire [England], January 13, 2011*. iPad drawing. Hockney has said about the iPad, 'It took me awhile to realize it's quite a serious tool you can use.'

Moleskine-sized sketchbook. He has brought attention to an important characteristic of these screens, writing: 'The fact that the screen is illuminated makes you choose luminous subjects.'[2]

The value of this particular technology lies in the hand's direct access to the screen through an electronic pencil or brush, which seems to restore the direct nervous impulse through them. Juhani Pallasmaa in his book *The Thinking Hand* has stated: 'The collaboration of the eye, hand and mind is crucial ... At its best the mental and material flow between the maker and the work is so tantalising that the work seems to be producing itself.'[3] So with the development of technology, which has allowed digital tools to become something akin to physical ones, like a pencil or brush, the computer may cease to be considered an anti-drawing, anti-painting machine. This introduction of tactility to drawing with the computer has changed our relationship to the screen, where the movement of our fingers now produces the lines translated by the electronic tools of line thicknesses and colours that respond directly to the physical movement of our hands. The hand and the eye are connected again, it is the movement of the finger which registers on the screen.

One interesting trajectory for experimentation with digital drawings is to take up hand-drawing techniques and transform them by computing. In the two examples of the rendering of the same space, a linear park in New Haven, Connecticut, in one case the looser line jottings used when producing a shaded drawing are converted into an algorithm changing its scale to create depth; in the other example the dot matrix language transforms the dots into squares.

The great weakness of current computer renderings is their flatness; they favour patterns and have difficulty presenting the third dimension – a battle that painting has spent centuries trying to overcome. Several computing programs have been developed in an attempt to resolve this issue, but that promise has not yet been fulfilled.

That said, the tactile experience of the apps for drawing directly on the computer screen using fingers is nowhere as satisfying as drawing and painting with pencil and brush on paper. The glass surface on which you work is not pleasant and is not a good interface. There is not, at least for me, the same level of control. However, when I look at the drawings Hockney has done on his iPhone or iPad, I can see that he has achieved a high level of precision. So that is clearly possible, and depends on individual ability and constant practice.

Still, the medium is not the basis for the pleasure in drawing. It can undoubtedly contribute to it, but the pleasure lies elsewhere. It comes from the deep concentration essential to the act of drawing; from the intense looking that produces interior quiet and an imagined silence around you, blocking out everything else; and from the feeling of your nerves and muscles as you attempt to capture whatever it is out there that you are after. The physical response to what you look at is vital; it activates the seeing, and you don't see as much without it. It is in the interaction between intense observation and the hand which tries to interpret what is being observed, editing and shaping it in the process,

that the pleasure of drawing or painting lies. This seems to imply that you draw what you see. That is not the case; you interpret what you see, editing, cutting out everything you are not interested in, distorting also in order to give the feeling of what is important apart from what is being seen. Drawing is an ideal tool to observe a site. But quite beyond that it is also a way of taking a plunge into ideas about the site.

But if the act of creating an image by hand is more important than the medium, why is it that I have made a strong case for the fundamental and enduring connection between painting and

Balmori Associates, Farmington Canal Greenway, New Haven, Connecticut, USA, 2009. Digital rendering. This combined perspective transforms hand-drawing techniques through digital mechanisms.

landscape design? It is because the medium makes a difference in *how* you make sense of what is around you. Each discipline – drawing by hand, painting by hand, computer drawing, computer painting – offers you a different way to interpret reality. Each speaks through you in its own language. However, *in spite of* their profound differences, each medium requires tremendous concentration and produces the great quietness and deep observation that lie at the heart of the act of drawing.

In other words, the result of what I like to call my 'lookings' will be very different if I am drawing with a pencil or pen, if I am painting with a brush, or if I am using my fingers on a computer screen. The difference even begins with what I select to draw; certain things are captured better by one medium than by another. Therefore, the connection of landscape to painting is not just an interesting historical fact. It matters a great deal. Whether you use this medium or that, affects content and the way the subject is interpreted. That landscape emerged from the representation of landscapes painted in oil had an effect on the landscapes subsequently designed. In addition landscape painting – thought to be dead after art moved from realism to abstraction – is reappearing in many guises and taking on a new life. As will be seen from examples of contemporary work discussed later, there is still a strong connection between painting and landscape architecture.

Drawing as Facilitator

Though the pleasure derived from drawing is something that feeds into a designer's creativity, ultimately it is part of a longer process in which ideas about a site are presented to non-designers, a client, or a public. The initial drawing stage is part of what enables a project, moving from observing and interpreting to concept and visualisation of that concept for the client and the users.

Drawing, at least to me, is part of the warp and woof of the design of landscape, but not just as the drawing at the end of the design process, when the finished design becomes public; it is an integral part of the entire process. Drawing is also a facilitator, as it was for a project for a linear park in New Haven, Connecticut. A group called Friends of the Farmington Canal contacted me about an old canal that had been abandoned and became a railroad that was now being abandoned in turn. This citizens' group knew that there were plans to sell off pieces of that land, and they wanted to preserve it and make it into a linear park for pedestrians, hikers and cyclists. The property as a whole extended up to Massachusetts – about 80 miles (130 kilometres) in total – but the Friends of the Farmington Canal were interested in only the first 14 miles (23 kilometres) of it. They had talked to numerous city and state officials and to the railroad owners, but the group could not seem to make any progress in convincing them to support the project. Some of the leaders of the group then got together and asked if I would produce some drawings to show the feasibility of creating a linear park on the site. They obtained a small grant from the National Endowment for the Arts (NEA) to fund the drawings, which I made over a period of three months. When the drawings were completed, the group held a new series of meetings with the government and railway officials and with many other interested citizens from whom, with the help of the drawings, they had now gained support. Nancy Alderman, who was the Chair of the Farmington Canal Rail-to-Trail Association, the NGO community group, later said that the drawings were critical to making their proposal go ahead.

The drawings were the facilitator; they were a tool of persuasion. With them, the group's idea no longer seemed just a pipe dream but instead became a feasible plan – and then a reality. Once there was a critical mass of people with sufficient conviction, they in turn were able to convince some of the officials to support the development of the linear park. As a result, the Friends of the Farmington Canal were able to make a deal with the Trust for Public Land to negotiate with the railroad for the property.

These are all different facets of drawing, the pleasure derived from it, the action of drawing and with what, and finally the altogether different aspect, when done professionally, of the effect it has on others.

References

1 André Le Nôtre (1613–1700) laid out the formal gardens at the Château de Chantilly in Picardy, northern France.
2 From an article by Martin Gayford published 20 October 2010 in *The Telegraph*: <http://www.hockneypictures.com/articles_html/2010/10-20-10.html>.

3 Juhani Pallasmaa, *The Thinking Hand: Existential and Embodied Wisdom in Architecture*, John Wiley & Sons (Chichester, UK), 2009.

Notebooks, Early Sketches and Late Drawings

3

To observe representation in the design process I have chosen three formats: notebooks which are the more private notations of a practitioner; the first sketches of a project, which is when an idea is put on paper; and the final representations of a project (renderings, diagrams, etc) – what is necessary to convey the final worked-out idea to the client and the public. Then I have chosen seven practices that are of particular interest in the diversity of their approaches and provide a wide gamut as well as a close-up examination of issues of representation. These close-ups are presented in Chapter 4.

A look at the contemporary scene and its practitioners and their forms of representing landscapes will show the break with established practice and give a hint of the new. The practitioners in this new stage of landscape architecture have two major issues to confront: the shift in the understanding of nature, in particular the role of change, and the change of scale in the work (see Chapter 2). But this look at the three kinds of drawings also uses historical examples, particularly in the notebook section, when notebooks, before photography and with early travel, were important visual references.

Notebooks

To reiterate, I draw in order to see. This kind of drawing, the 'seeing' drawing, is done in notebooks. It is drawing done as play. These drawings are fundamentally different from the targeted project-driven drawings done in the office, yet both are joined by the maker of the drawing. The professional drawings are social, they are discussed, shared, critiqued by everybody in the office. The notebook

William Gilpin, 'An intersection, where one piece of the ground falls into another, and at the bottom you see the basin of the valley', 1775. Ink on paper. Part of Gilpin's notebook of the Western Tour, this drawing integrates text with a detailed ink and watercolour depiction of the landscape.

drawing language. They are notes or notations on what you are seeing. Things you would like to annotate. It is as if you were writing notes and when doing that you don't worry about the choice of font, just what is being written. William Gilpin's travel notebook drawings are sometimes annotated with text. Peter Shepheard's meeting agenda is covered with doodles.

drawing is done as a solitary action. In most cases it is not for show. What is clear is that notebook drawing is common among design professionals and that the drawings have their own character, are fun to look at and much more individual. They are also part of the story of landscape drawing and should be considered as part of the story of representation.

Although they are not overtly part of the actual design of a landscape, the drawings are an important part of the creative process. As a whole they are playful, they are not trying to make a statement, they are observations. They use a more conventional

The more adventurous drawing comes in trying to represent a landscape not yet created, with no reality but that of its drawings, as Samuel Palmer's notebook illustrates with fantastic trees and vegetation as well as a realistic agricultural landscape thrown in, including a note about making neat memorandums and putting them on the overleaf.

So what do landscape architects draw in their notebooks? Landscapes – certainly Dan Kiley's sketch of a few black magic-marker lines shows the power of a deeply shaded place created by allées of large canopied trees. Large vistas or small details – a plant, an outdoor step, water and its movement – appear in Lawrence Halprin's notebook (more notebook drawings by Lawrence Halprin are in Chapter 4). A rock, in Elizabeth Mead's 'Signature Rock', is placed on the gutter which gives tension to the drawing, as if a weight were placed on the pages. And land patterns from an airplane depict Kenneth Helphand's flight from San Francisco to Portland. Laurie Olin's Cascade Mountains drawing is a reminder of how much notebook drawing is done while travelling.

There are few general points to be made about the subject. Two should be mentioned: the use of specific media in different time periods and preferred themes. There are usually favourite themes, in my case, the sea, the desert, and above all, the light of the sky, and how it plays out on different surfaces. Lawrence Halprin's notebooks are about Oregon's High Sierra mountains and streams, and myriad iterations of rocky profiles and water movement fill the pages.

The materials used often mark an era: the popularity of watercolours in the 19th century, the magic markers of the 20th century, the yellow trace of the 1960s, the soft 6 to 10B lead of certain periods, the HB lead of others.

Why include notebooks since they are personal, non-classifiable, and separate from professional drawings? Here I have to emphasise the importance they have for me as a professional; there is something important to my work in them, yet it is not a direct

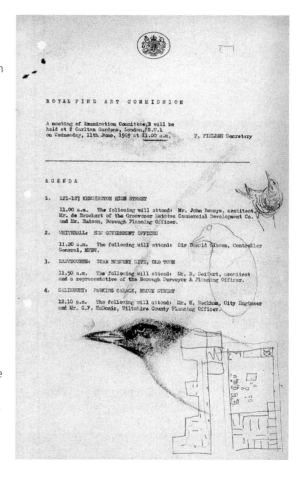

Peter Shepheard, sketches on a meeting agenda, 1969. Typewritten notes with ink sketches on paper.
On this meeting agenda from a Royal Fine Arts Commission meeting held on 11 June 1969, Shepheard doodled three birds and a plan.

transfer. But they are connected, they are life-giving, they are important.

Here are some observations on their import, which include my own thoughts and those of others. Perhaps it is the state of concentration that they engender, sometimes setting off musings about the landscape you are observing or about the design of a landscape. Recording a drawing in a notebook allows you to understand the particularities of an element in the landscape, for example the movement of currents marked by subtle changes in the water's surface reflectivity. In other words, the impact of notebooks is

in how they inspire new ways of seeing and also in the state of concentration the activity of drawing engenders.

When I travel, I always take a small Moleskine notebook with me, and drawing in it is the most rewarding activity of the trip. It is the vehicle by which I absorb all the newness that the journey uncovers. When I travel with students I require them to bring a notebook and – no matter how attached they are to their cameras – to make drawings in addition to taking photographs. I've noticed that when students work with a camera, they move about restlessly all the time and are soon ready to move on. But drawing slows them down and they sit very quietly – sometimes for hours – and seem to take in the space and rest within it. I stress that I don't expect them to create a finished product; instead, I expect them to

**Elizabeth Mead, Signature
Rock – Wyoming, Wyoming,
USA, 2012. Watercolour on
paper.**
The artist Elizabeth Mead
places her drawing of a rock on
the notebook's gutter.

observe and to see, rather than to focus on making
the drawing look good to present it to me. Drawing
is never a copying exercise or an exact rendering of
anything. It is a creative endeavour of interpreting

what is before your eyes by ignoring some aspects of
what you are seeing while stressing others, at times
synthesising, at times exaggerating, and ultimately
rendering an imaginary place.

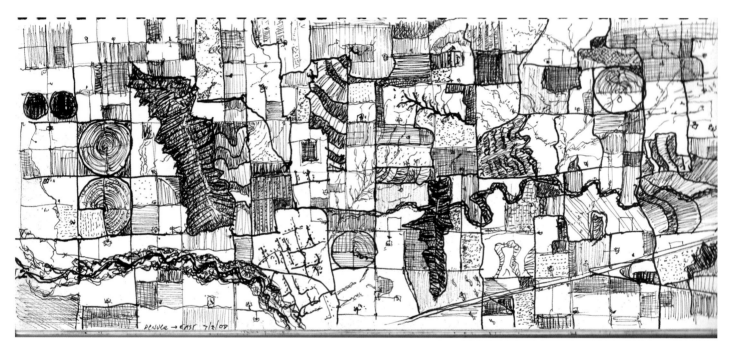

Kenneth Helphand, Denver – East 7/2/08, Colorado, USA. Pen on paper.
Helphand routinely draws what he sees out of the airplane window. Noting the duration, direction and date of his travel, his primary interest is in describing the topological patterns that he observes.

The pleasure I derive from my own notebook drawings is closely followed by that I get looking at the notebook drawings of others. The examples that I've selected are here in part because of the pleasure they give. And because they are playful. And because they are in some way connected to our professional work, though in what ways is a personal matter. In my case, they make me see the landscape and see what I couldn't see in a glance or a photograph. The thorough concentration in looking and trying to capture what I am seeing in that looking is where the notebooks play their role.

Like the first sketches in a design, which will be examined further on, notebooks blend the inner and outer world, and in that way they are somewhat magical. There is a mystique about notebooks among

Laurie Olin, Sauk River Farm on steelhead fishing trip near the Cascade Mountains, Washington, USA, 1967. Pen on paper.
Olin uses loose lines and different media to document a fishing trip in Washington.

writers, particularly among anthropologists and their field notes (field notes do involve drawing). Michael Taussig has discussed the fieldwork notebook as an 'outrigger of the soul'.[1] The anthropologist Jean Jackson has recorded the irrational responses of cultural anthropologists about their field notes in her essay 'I am a Fieldnote'.[2] Reading both Taussig and Jackson, I recognise similar responses in my own notebooks. As Taussig says, 'even looking at somebody else's drawing, I am likely to stretch out my hand to the thing pictured. Speaking for myself, I rarely have this feeling with a photograph. Drawings are Dionysiac.'

An emotional attachment to the things drawn, and a sense of comfort deriving from the notebook

Diana Balmori, water reflections, Branford, Connecticut, USA, 2001. Crayon.
Surface motion, background reflections.

photography would need another separate discussion, that understanding is valuable.

Drawing does bring about closeness with the thing drawn, it is akin to a friendship.

Notebooks, Joan Didion has said, have nothing to do with a factual record. In her essay 'On Keeping a Notebook', she sees a common thread among all those fragments of perception. Though she is referring to written notes, there is an equivalence for designers, drawings are the way designers take notes. They strike a chord, she says, and that chord is the author's life which keeps changing, as do all lives. These fragments keep us in touch with our former selves 'and I suppose that keeping in touch is what notebooks are all about'.[3]

Still another trait about notebooks is how most of us use them mainly when travelling. I have explained this to myself as this being the only time I have for drawing. But I am not sure that is all there is to it. In travelling you are confronted with many new unexpected images which move you and you are eager to observe them, to draw them.

The two examples I gave earlier from my notebooks were of drawings done at leisure and in colour. They require some time, 30 minutes to an hour, usually depending on the size. Much more frequently I produce simple line sketches done on the go and in a small notebook with a soft lead pencil, sometimes a thin pen. The pencil-line sketches have a very particular role, they are truly 'looking' exercises, they make you

drawings, may add to the mysticism surrounding them, but they are true experiences mentioned by others which I share. Taussig asked: so why not use a photograph, instead of a drawing or as well as a drawing? 'Photography is taking, drawing is making' is his response. And though the dialogue with

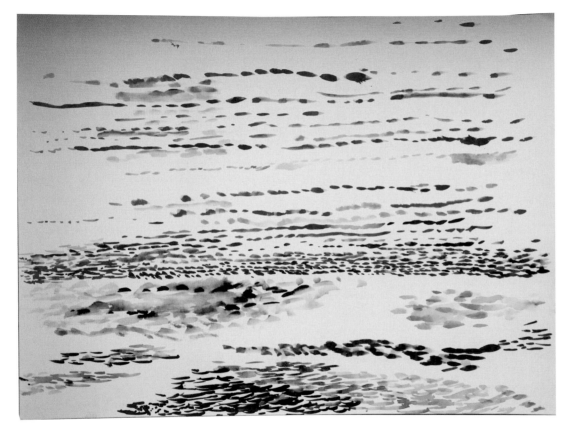

Diana Balmori, water reflections, Branford, Connecticut, USA, 2001. Watercolour.
Surface motion, surface stillness.

look and because of the quickness of the sketch they make you make quick decisions about what is most important. For painters they are preparatory, they precede a final painting. But for those of us who are not painters they are not preparatory exercises, they are 'looking' exercises. They make us look at a landscape

Diana Balmori, London, England, 2008. Lead pencil. While a colour pencil sketch might take 30 minutes to an hour to make, this drawing was created in seconds in a small pocket notebook.

and catch a quality or feature of it which we have decided is important to us.

The sketch is done rapidly. It is meant to capture broad outlines, not details. Five or 10 minutes as a rule of thumb. That immediately makes you create a hierarchy in what you are looking at, what is most important in it, what it is that has brought your eye to look at this place and not another. It may be

successful or not as a sketch, but it has succeeded in understanding what counts.

Watercolours for me have very much the spirit of the sketch. Watercolour is a fast medium, it flows. You can't stop once you've started and you can't correct. It has the freshness of something glanced at and captured in an instant. But it is a difficult medium requiring much preparation and equipment. Watercolours by masters like JMW Turner (1775–1851) have much the spirit of the sketch. They are Turner's way of sketching. The word he uses for his sketches is 'Beginnings'. And this has been interpreted as meaning that it is a study for an oil painting. I would interpret it as a beginning sketch which captures the most important features. And a sketch really is a beginning. It is the first look and synthesis, and it starts with the looking. I call my own sketches 'lookings'.

Today we honour the glance, the immediate response, the catching of something on the wind. And in particular we value capturing something with a human gesture, with the mark of the pencil or of the watercolour brush showing the hand doing it. Because of the speed of the delivery, these gestures have an energy and child-like quality to them, also a roughness and unfinished aspect. To the untrained eye they may seem worthless, the work of an amateur or of someone just learning to draw. But if you consider the work of William Kent (1685–1748), for example, a man who designed landscapes and buildings in the early

18th century, you have drawings with some of these same qualities. They are crude, surprisingly so, but Kent's drawings have immediacy, they study an idea rather than display a final product. He has dogs in the drawings, beggars, horse riders, all with an unfinished quality that makes you look at them as a sketch, placing him closer to our own era.

What do I put in notebooks? Landscapes that have a large horizontal expanse, for which notebooks in a landscape format are ideally suited, invite you to engage with them. The landscape format also allows you to expand the horizontal dimension by using two facing pages. What interests me in this is the variation of colour that different parts of the landscape have as you displace your view horizontally, particularly if it is a water surface which is so sensitive to the light from the sky above as in *Changing Sky and Sea, Nantucket.* And as in *Choppy Sea, Miami, Florida:* a quick sketch to catch an instantaneous form that dissolves and changes before you have even started drawing, as a detail of the surface of water and its motion.

The virtue of watercolour is, in my case, the rapid impression of colour. It is not a medium for details, though painters and also 19th-century landscape renderers have indeed used it as such. Watercolour is exquisite for the splash of colour, for

Diana Balmori, 4pm, Nantucket, Massachusetts, USA, 2010. Lead pencil. Waves, stormy afternoon.

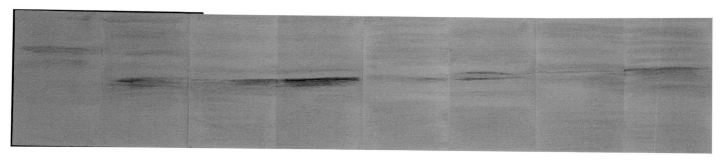

Diana Balmori, changing sky and sea, Nantucket, Massachusetts, USA, 2010. Coloured pencil.
Drawing in pencil under a tight time constraint makes you prioritise what is most important.

its transparency, and for its liquidity, so water-like. But most sketching is done on the go, on a walk, or from inside a car, and for that the graphite lead is the instrument at hand with the small notebook in the architect's inside jacket pocket. That is how you put down the feeling of a piece of city, or a large background landscape such as of mountains: big fat traces, no details, lines, mainly, in the hope it will reflect what that place says to you.

Finally, there are some quick sketches in my work that try to capture the idea of variegated, contrasting textures, outlines that are then converted into a collage following notations put on the drawing of the relative darkness and lightness of the different parts.

Diana Balmori, choppy sea, Miami, Florida, USA, 2013. Coloured pencil.
Swiftly sketched, this drawing attempts to capture the volatility of colour.

Early sketches

The early sketch is an idea jotted down at the beginning of creating a design; often it is a mere scribble, a notation in drawn form that sets a direction. At times that sketch is the basis for the next step; in other instances, the idea may prove uninteresting or impossible and is abandoned, and then another sketch is tried. The early sketch shows a rougher, more abstract side of drawing; it interests me, above all, because it is an attempt to represent the conceptual ideas at the outset of a project. The late drawing presents a developed idea and in most cases is a 3D rendering. Two examples of these two stages of

representation, viewed together, illustrate how the original idea can be transformed, in some cases even lost, in going from a first impulse to a detailed design.

This early sketch by Martha Schwartz for Master Designer's Garden Plot 6 for an exhibition in Xi'an, China, is of a sculptural dug-out space for people to explore, and shows exactly the kind of playfulness that you expect from these early sketches. The final rendering has the desired quality of the space, but it has clearly been simplified, as often occurs along the journey from initial idea to final design.

Another example of an early drawing that is simple and also informally conveys both the character

Diana Balmori, Nantucket, Massachusetts, USA, 2009. Watercolour.
The medium of watercolour is a means of expeditiously conveying the impression of colour.

Diana Balmori, Miami, Florida, USA, 2006. Watercolour.
The diaphanous and liquid quality of watercolour expresses sensations difficult to transmit by pencil.

Diana Balmori, sky, London, England, 2005. Watercolour.
Watercolour ties together the fluidity with the rapidity of the medium.

of a landscape and a landscape design process is the sketch for Qunli Stormwater Park's 'Green Sponge for a Water-Resilient City' in Harbin City, China, by Kongjian Yu. Yu, the founder of Turenscape, views the story of the emperor who 'helped the rice grow' as an allegory for our time. The emperor planted rice, but thought the plants were growing too slowly, so he started tugging the shoots up to hurry them, killing them in the process. Yu has stated that his aim in designing a landscape is to allow people living in cities to reconnect with the experience of how things grow. His landscapes can at times be confused with agricultural sites. His drawing

for Qunli presents both the overall plan and individual sections, showing how the water is gathered and absorbed as a result of the shaping of the terrain, and then made to flow around the edges of the site, where it is cleansed. This early sketch, like Schwartz's, conveys a more dynamic view than that of the final rendering.

The early sketch is the most difficult stage of a design to capture. It reflects the first moment of thinking about the brief for the project and the initial idea about what form it can take and how it can work. It embodies the transition from abstract idea to concrete design. There is often no record of that

process because at this stage the idea is so preliminary and incomplete, and the sketch of it so rough, that it doesn't seem to be worth keeping. So piles of paper go into the recycling bin from this kind of initial design session. This became evident to me when I looked in my office for examples of this stage and realised how much we had thrown away. In addition, many early ideas are rejected even before they begin to be developed, which increases the vulnerability of the record of this stage. The first sketch is akin to (but

Diana Balmori, Central Park, New York City, New York, USA, 2011. Collage.
Juxtaposition of patterned papers to diminish importance of the edges.

generally not the same as) the Beaux-Arts idea of the *parti* – loosely translated into English as 'scheme'. Design sketches are often created earlier and are less formalised and less complete; *parti* implies having a vision of the whole, while the initial sketch may reflect only one aspect of the full design, or capture just a small idea, which may ultimately turn into a concept of the whole project. When an early sketch itself represents a concept of the whole, it truly is a *parti*.

Capturing an idea in a freehand drawing, where the thinking takes over and the desire to give it form with the pencil is secondary, is much like thinking out loud. Such a sketch says something instantly about an idea; it is the best conveyor of thought, resulting from a tug of war where the lines are trying to catch that thought, sometimes taking on a life of their own. At times this yields unexpected – even surprising – results, some valuable, others that have lost their way. This does not make for pretty drawings, or for drawings at all, really. They are not even containers of thought – just foggy outlines of it. These early sketches are not unlike notebook drawings, but those usually try to capture something you are seeing. As you sketch, the pencil drops what's going on in your mind onto the page, leaving out everything that makes drawings understandable. There is usually nothing recognisable there, except to the person

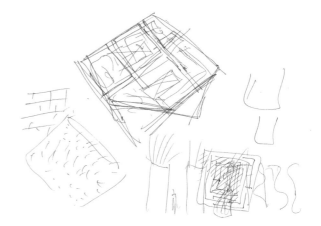

Martha Schwartz Partners, early sketch for Master Designer's Garden Plot 6, Xi'an, China, 2011. Pen on paper.
MSP was invited to design a small garden installation on the theme of the harmonious co-existence of nature and the city for an exhibition in Xi'an, China. An early sketch for the project shows a sculptural, mysterious passage.

doing the drawing. They are not meant to be shown to anyone else. The pencil is desperately trying to get at something unformed, at great speed. It is obedient only to the thought. You start, sometimes stop, and then start over. Or you vertiginously dash after the idea, seeing if you can capture it, all the time either

Martha Schwartz, Xi'an International Horticultural Expo 2011, Master Designer's Garden Plot 6, Xi'an, China, 2011. Photoshop rendering. In a Photoshop representation of the same site as is drawn in the sketch on page 57, MSP composed the garden with four elements: corridors of traditional grey brick walls and paving, willow trees, mirrors and bronze bells.

Kongjian Yu / Turenscape, sketch of a 'green sponge for a water-resilient city' – Qunli Stormwater Park, Harbin City, Heilongjiang Province, China, 2009. Coloured marker on paper.

This sketch shows Kongjian Yu's concept for the park as a green sponge, meant to cleanse and store urban stormwater.

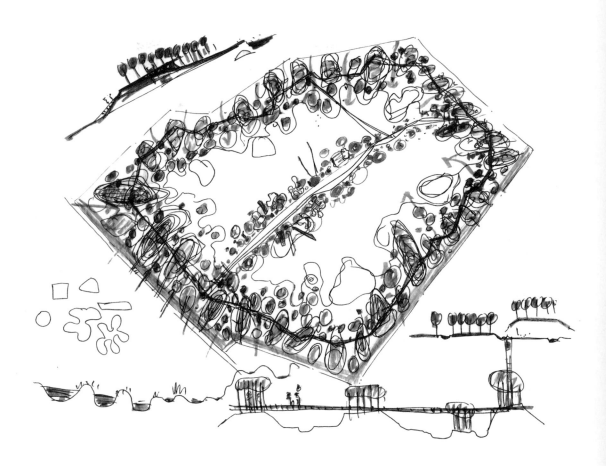

Kongjian Yu / Turenscape, aerial rendering of a 'green sponge for a water-resilient city' – Qunli Stormwater Park, Harbin City, Heilongjiang Province, China, 2009. Digital rendering.
What Kongjian Yu describes as 'ecosystem services' – the protection of native habitats, aquifer recharge, recreational use and aesthetic experience – are combined in Qunli Stormwater Park as a means of fostering urban development.

eliminating things and saying no, not that, it is not that, or instead getting at something that seems accurately to reflect the idea.

There is certainly no direct route from the initial sketch to the final rendering. Sometimes coloured pencils or pastels are later used on the original drawing to differentiate surfaces. Sometimes outlines are drawn on a photomontage of the site. Sometimes, a diagram of the initial idea is superimposed on a computer drawing of the site plan; in some ways, this is similar to the 17th- and 18th-century practice of drawing an outline on the landscaper's survey. But the very first stage is the most difficult to capture; its drawings are enigmatic, on the whole, and speak only to those with knowledge of the design problem. I consider them some of the most interesting drawings of the process, produced as a previously unexpressed idea makes its first appearance. It is the most challenging

William Wordsworth, signed letter to Lady Beaumont, 23 December 1806. Ink on paper.
This informal plan of a winter garden at Coleorton Hall, the seat of Sir George Beaumont in Leicestershire, England, was embedded in a letter sent to Lady Beaumont. The sonnet was addressed to her as well.

moment, putting creativity to the test. It requires concentration and thinking, and then finding a way to represent that thinking. It is a magical moment, when a completely invisible, interior process emerges as a set of lines on a surface.

Though the roles and subjects of design drawings in different eras vary enormously, crude early sketches can be found during each historical period. It should be stressed that in the 17th century, design drawings were infrequent; Humphry Repton, for example, is said never to have drawn plans. But we do find early examples of bare-bones drawings, some of them annotated to make them readable as well as to make the designer's intention clear to other people. Although the poet William Wordsworth was not a landscaper, he was commissioned to come up with ideas for a winter garden and annotated his sketch extensively.

A sketch can be very spare but still convey one overriding idea; indeed, presenting the main design concept in a simple form is what these early sketches do best. For example, in this outline of a design for John Danvers's house from 1691, a space is shaped into an oval through the location of trees. In a letter to George John Legh in 1797, Repton sketched the possible design for a space at an intersection of roads in a small town. Two sketches by poet and garden designer Alexander Pope show us alternative treatments

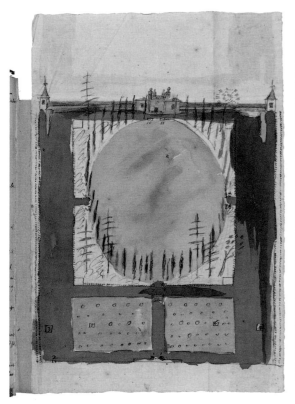

of the same area in a garden. Though produced at a more advanced stage of the design process, the contemporary drawing by Erik Dhont for the garden of a medieval bailiff's house at Gaasbeek is still a sketch, one that tries to put all the pieces of the design together in a simplified form. Snøhetta's sketch for the Edmonton Airport project makes a forested angled swale the central organisational idea of the whole

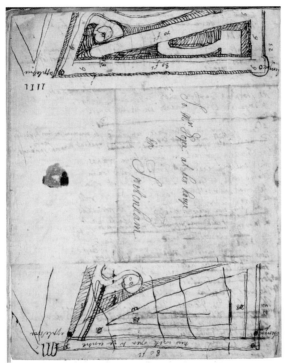

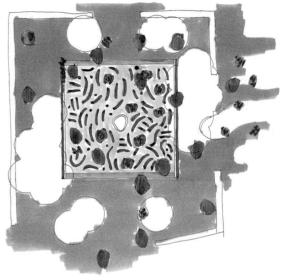

(Right) Alexander Pope, garden plans, two versions for the same area, undated. Ink on paper.
This drawing by Pope shows two possible interventions at the same garden.

(Far right) Erik Dhont, sketch for the garden of a medieval bailiff's house at Gaasbeek, Belgium, 1990–95. Ink and watercolour on paper.
The owner of the site asked Dhont to create a garden that would harmonise with the extant residence built in 1602. Dhont used a labyrinth and the *hortus conclusus* as historical referents, with the analogy slightly unhinged.

design. An early pencil sketch of Jeanne-Claude and Christo's *Over the River* shows their essential concept of creating a temporary light fabric cover over the Arkansas River in Colorado. (The project is still working its way through the various bureaucracies.)

Late drawings

The most social drawing of the design process is the final rendering. The driving force behind it is the need to persuade the client to select a particular design and go forward with it. Accordingly, the final rendering is meant to convince the client and whichever authorities need to approve the project that the design can – and should – be built. So these final drawings have to have a legibility which sometimes conflicts with the

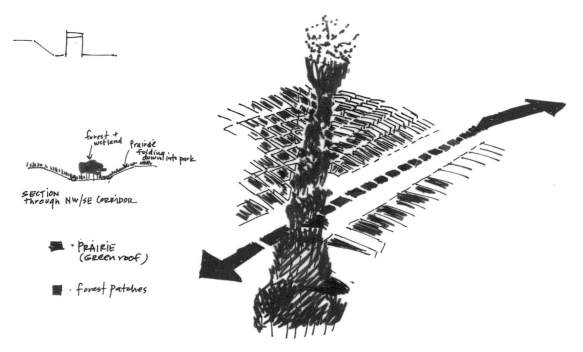

SECTION
through NW/SE CORRIDOR

forest + wetland
Prairie folding down into park

■ · PRAIRIE
(GREEN ROOF)

■ · forest patches

Snøhetta, sketch for Edmonton Airport, Alberta, Canada, 2011. Marker on paper.
As part of a competition for the redevelopment of the Edmonton City Centre Airport, Snøhetta proposed a design that integrated a green corridor into the airport complex.

designer's essential intention, as it usually requires an excessively explicit level of specificity to make the uses and possibilities of the design evident to the client and to the approval agencies. In other words, the drawings spell out too much, become overwrought and overly prescriptive, leaving little to the imagination. And

yet, you would like to leave that aspect of the design an open agenda that the user can both discover and reinterpret. Nonetheless, because the designer is then committed to the representation in each drawing, when these individual renderings are assembled for presentation, they dictate how the realised landscape

**Christo, *Over the River*
(project for approximately
six miles (10 kilometres) of
river), Colorado, USA, 1992.
Pencil on paper.**
For this work-in-progress by
Christo and Jeanne-Claude,
Christo drew luminous fabric
panels suspended for 5.9
miles (9.5 kilometres) over the
Arkansas River in south-central
Colorado.

will appear. Although their formats vary, all final renderings link landscape designer and client in a financial relationship based on a shared vision.

In *Art and Illusion* (1960), Ernst Gombrich argued against the idea that the goal of a depiction is to imitate visual appearances. Gombrich instead focuses on 'convincing representation' – visual representation as a constructive process, not a mimetic one.[4] Gombrich's insight is instructive for renderings because they communicate a vision of a potential future reality. More to his point, there is a disjunction between the marks on the page

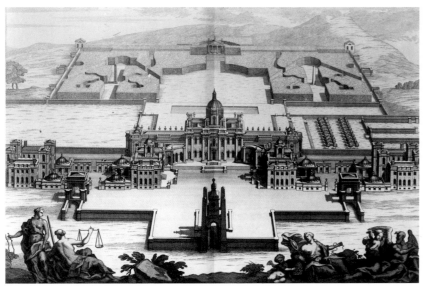

sketched in the same mode in which the architectural structure is rendered, or it might take the form of a perspective – which is arguably easier for the client to digest – thereby increasing the prospect of securing a commission. Historic renderings rarely portray the landscape in any form other than a plan or a perspective; cross sections and elevations are notably absent. The landscape surrounding Castle Howard is included in the accompanying unifying view, but lacks all detail.

and what might (or might not) be built from them in the actualised landscape. Here it may be important to take a look at some historical examples of rendering. What is striking about them is their consistency. The conventions they all generally follow include drawing both architectural structures and the landscape; sketching a unifying view that depicts at least large areas of the landscape, and sometimes shows the entire site; and showing plantings in generic terms, rather than in detail. The comprehensive rendering might be in the form of a plan, with the landscape

Many historical landscapes were rendered not by the designers themselves, but by an artist hired separately by the client to create a portrayal of the landscape after it was built. From the Renaissance through to the 18th century, clients commissioned painters or engravers such as Israel Silvestre, John Rocque, Johannes Kip, Leonard Knyff and Giovanni Battista Falda to compose those images.

Early unifying plans depicted essentially flat terrains, in which there is little sense of the landscape's natural or manipulated topography. By the 17th century, however, renderings began to use shading to indicate different aspects of the landscape, although only to a limited extent. Over time, there developed a more nuanced use of washes and shading to convey depth credibly. William Kent's renderings of Rousham (1737) were remarkable in the way large trees were grouped at assorted angles to intimate a generic sense of the landscape's topography. In these drawings, it was the edges and boundaries of the landscape that tended to be represented with a three-dimensional effect, which gave the interstitial areas a sense of flatness that might or might not be an analogue for the topography.

During the 19th century, the dominant mode of rendering shifted, reflecting a new cultural desire to convey information. Previously, large overviews representing the landscape as a unified structure dominated renderings. With the onset of scientific realism, as Jennifer Raab argues, the function and formal depiction of details that imparted knowledge changed.[5] Renderings assumed a new technical precision; they were used to depict sightlines, and text was inserted into the drawing itself. They also become more microscopic, perhaps reflecting a new phenomenological interest in drawing in a mode that encouraged the viewer to 'enter into' the simulacrum. The firm grip of the Picturesque also favoured the view of visitors on the ground and the variety of experiences they had in travelling through a garden.

In one of the first meetings of the Photographic Society of London, John Leighton complained that photographs were 'at present too literal to compete with works of art' and missed the opportunity to elevate the imagination.[6] In certain respects, this is also true of landscape representation. As the discipline moves closer to rejoining the family of the arts, this concern will be more critical and play a more dominant role in how landscape presents itself – although some will consider the role of art irrelevant to this professional encounter of client and designer and argue that the effort to create final drawings as works of art was a practice of an earlier era. However, those historical landscape paintings and engravings were produced after the project was finished. Final renderings today serve a different purpose.

The 20th century has produced some famous renderers, who were commissioned by designers' offices to create the visionary iconic image of a project. However, these renderers tended to work in architecture rather than in landscape design, partly because of the weakness of the discipline of landscape architecture at that time. Many of them were free agents who worked exclusively on renderings. Professional organisations for architectural renderers, including the Japanese Architectural Renderers Association and Britain's Society of Architectural Illustration, were also established. In the United States, the most famous renderer was Hugh Ferriss, an extraordinary artistic draughtsman. Jules Guérin, Carlos Diniz, Steve Oles and Frank Constantino are also well-known 20th-century renderers. Some offices had a superb renderer in-house; one of Eero Saarinen's early partners, Jay Barr, was such a figure. A person of particular interest for landscape architecture is Marion Mahony, one of the designers in Frank Lloyd Wright's office, who was also the renderer of many of Wright's projects. Mahony had a particularly felicitous ability for giving landscape an important presence in the design. In the smaller landscape offices of the 20th century, the principals produced the renderings. The best examples of these are Laurie Olin's drawings and Lawrence Halprin's colour felt-pen renderings.

Final renderings continue to dominate design presentations. Those created in-house in a design office are quite different from those produced by firms or individuals who specialise exclusively in renderings. With the advent of the computer in the late 20th and early 21st centuries, outsourcing has become

Carl Theodor Sørensen, musical garden, 1958. Pencil on paper.
Sørensen typically did not draw in perspective, but would create minimal plans indicating the concept behind a design idea.

(Opposite) James Wines, Best Forest Building, Richmond, Virginia, USA, 1978. Pen and ink on paper.
Wines's Best Forest Building in west Richmond was designed to allow the extant wooded area to coexist with the constructed building and give the impression that the forest is recovering its lost ground.

BEST RICHMOND SHOWROOM

WORK SITE 1988

prevalent, in part because work done by foreign rendering firms costs much less. But the results are extremely homogeneous.

Today it is the designers themselves, rather than the clients, who hire others to produce renderings. The designs are sent out to computer rendering companies – usually run by young architects or draughtspeople seeking sources of extra income – which produce commercial images. Though there is a back-and-forth between the designer's and the renderer's office, the pressure of time makes the modifications minimal. In general, images produced by such rendering companies are hyperrealistic. They use brilliant colours and tend to fill the designed space with the same banal details – children with balloons, joggers, store signs, sunsets and usually lots of people – to indicate how heavily the space will be used and how popular it will be.

In contrast, some examples of work done by individual renderers – from the abstract and geometric hedge garden by Carl Theodor Sørensen (1958) to James Wines's Best Forest Building – give a sense of the variety of media and approaches used. Because of his facility with pen and pencil, Wines, the founder of SITE, can at times design and draw simultaneously, creating compelling initial drawings that look like – and can serve as – final renderings. A sculptor who went on to work with architects, Wines was a pioneer in raising the

Adriaan van Haaften, central perspective at eye level, courtyard garden, arboretum, Wageningen, the Netherlands, 2008. Coloured pencil and ink on paper.
Van Haaften decided to colour this drawing only partially, creating an image that is both a perspective and a line drawing, made for an arboretum in the Netherlands.

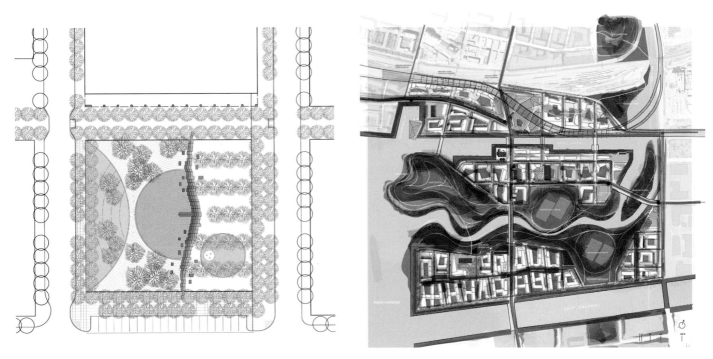

(Above right) Michael Van Valkenburgh, Lower Don Lands, Toronto, Canada, 2007 – ongoing. Rendered plan.
In this drawing, the artificial topography of the landscape is heightened.

issue of the integration of architecture and landscape. At a time when those disciplines were treated as totally separate fields, he balanced his project for the Best Products stores on an edgy border between the two; politically double-edged too is his take on American retail. It was a bold and pioneering proposal for the 1970s and it is surprising that he succeeded in getting the project built. His drawings are artistic in the best sense of the word. They stand on the border between early sketches and late drawings, just as his designs occupy a position between landscape and architecture.

A partially coloured frontal view of a garden by Adriaan van Haaften (2008) plays with the juxtaposition between the crisp black-and-white lines

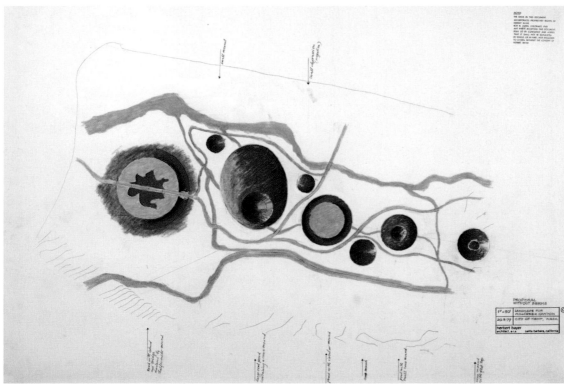

in one area of the rendering and shaded drawing in coloured pencil in another, making the effect of the use of the contrasting drawings evident. Peter Walker & Partners' rendition of the design for Jamison Square in Portland uses concentrated and subtle colouring to make the plan seem nearly three-dimensional. In addition, the rendering is extremely artistic, which is a rare quality in a plan.

Landscape representation is in an ongoing battle to free itself from the Picturesque. One such effort is

Chip Sullivan, plan and perspective for his own garden, 1992. Watercolour over pen and ink on Arches 140lb watercolour paper. Sullivan's rendering shows a trompe-l'oeil perspective on the far wall of the garden's central axis.

Michael Van Valkenburgh's rendered plan for the Lower Don Lands in Toronto, Canada, which intentionally exaggerates the naturalism of the design and makes it obvious that the mounds are human-made. He uses the same strategy in his Wellesley project and in Teardrop Park which, in his words, 'evokes the physical power of geology and plate tectonics without attempting to hide its origins as a constructed object'.[7]

For Herbert Bayer's landscape for Mill Creek Canyon – perhaps the very first instance of ecological function being used to create form – coloured pencil drawings were made to present to the town commissioners. These unpublished renderings are preserved in the town's archives. A simplified version of the design was selected and built in 1982. Chip Sullivan's drawing for his own garden is a compelling integration of plan and perspective into a single rendering that speaks of late 20th-century commercial art forms, such as those of Peter Max, as well as of Pop Art.

In my own work I have found the section taking on a leading role, and I suspect that in our new focus on coastlines and rising sea levels the section will become much more important. The work of Anuradha Mathur and Dilip da Cunha is a valuable example of this use of the section.

They propose a distinctly different approach to the representation of the late stage: 'Design in an estuary must begin with a new visualization. The view from above has privileged land over the waters of an estuary ... As such the Mumbai flood of 2005 (and the rise in sea levels expected over the next decades) demands more than analyses and solutions. It calls for a change in the way Mumbai's terrain is seen ... It changes the primary vehicle of visual representation of Mumbai from plan to section.'[8] Their illustration of the terrain as a series of sections of all of Mumbai is also a significant achievement in aesthetic terms. Their work as a whole turns around the management of water in the landscape and they propose the section as the definitive representation in those landscapes. Their own rationale for this is a direct response to the issue of constant change: 'To seek stability – to settle – is a human condition. For design practice it is important to respond to this need as a negotiated tension between the desire for settlement and the inevitability of change. One way is to construct boundaries, material or representational, and aim to separate, control, predict and manage what's within. Another way is to construct what we call anchors in an open, mutable field – a process that begins with material specificity but extends in ways we cannot entirely predict. Today, sadly, the former approach dominates design and planning.'[9]

Anuradha Mathur + Dilip da Cunha, sections of Mumbai, India 2009. Digital rendering.
In response to self-posed questions such as 'what is a river' or 'what is a city', Mathur and da Cunha have developed a form of sectional drawing that they call 'photoworks' and 'photowalks'. This drawing shows the estuary of Mumbai through sections.

References

1 Michael Taussig, *I Swear I Saw This: Drawings in Fieldwork Notebooks, Namely My Own*, University of Chicago Press (Chicago), 2011.
2 Jean Jackson, '"I am a Fieldnote": Fieldnotes as a Symbol of Professional Identity', in Roger Sanjek (ed), *Fieldnotes: The Makings of Anthropology*, Cornell University Press (Ithaca), 1990, pp 3–33.
3 Joan Didion, 'On Keeping a Notebook', in *Slouching towards Bethlehem*, Farrar, Straus and Giroux (New York), 1968.
4 Ernst Gombrich, *Art and Illusion; A Study in the Psychology of Pictorial Representation*, Pantheon Books (New York), 1960.
5 Jennifer Raab, *The Art and Science of Detail: Frederic Church and Nineteenth-Century Landscape Painting* (book project).
6 Hope Kingsley, 'An Axis Between Old and New' in *Seduced by Art: Photography Past and Present*, National Gallery (London), 2013, p 17.
7 J Green, 'Interview with Michael Van Valkenburgh', *The Dirt*, web, 13 October 2010 ‹http://dirt.asla.org›.
8 Anuradha Mathur and Dilip da Cunha, *Soak: Mumbai in an Estuary*, Rupa & Co (New Delhi), 2009, p 93.
9 Nicolas Pevzner and Sanjukta Sen, 'Preparing Ground: An Interview with Anuradha Mathur + Dilip da Cunha', *Design Observer*, 29 June 2010.

4

Contemporary Landscape Architects and Landscape Artists

Consider now taking seven short journeys through drawn landscapes in the company of their authors, and as you do, follow the thread of each creator's design intent and view of nature – which are the critical elements in their decisions about landscape representation. This small group – Landscape Urbanists, Bernard Lassus, Patricia Johanson, Richard Haag, Stig Andersson, Lawrence Halprin, and my own work – has been selected because of the different approach each practitioner offers. The drawings discussed are not intended to describe all that is happening in the field today; instead, the selection is focused on explorations of new languages, more appropriate to the contemporary situation. These approaches break away from traditional forms and seem to open doors to a different practice that is congruent with a new view of nature. Some do this by representing process over time, some by representing representation, some by representing a nature in which humans and all other living things are equally important, and some by seeking a new artistic language for the landscape. A critical element that must be kept in mind is how difficult it is to represent landscape. In the following chapter, I describe various historical attempts to solve this problem. They may shed some light on the challenges involved.

Landscape architecture is an art of peripheral vision. Peripheral vision is essential for appreciating and understanding landscape; central vision alone cannot capture it. To explore this, vision scientist Denis Pelli, professor of psychology and neuroscience at New York University, and I set up an experiment to measure how varying the scope of an observer's field of view affects the observer's experience of the beauty of a landscape.

We adopted George Santayana's (1896) definition of beauty: the pleasure we attribute to an object.[1]

The experiment was conducted as follows: at 3.30pm on 23 April 2010, two observers stood in Hudson River Park at 14th Street in New York City, looking west at the Hudson River and the New Jersey coastline. The observers viewed the scene before them with various restrictions of their fields of view. With both eyes unrestricted, the observer's field of view was approximately 210°; with just one eye, (closing the other), the field of was roughly 160°. Looking

through a paper tube further restricted the field of view. Various lengths of the paper tube restricted the field of view down to 57°, 17° or 6°. Each observer was asked to rate the pleasure of viewing the scene, on a scale from zero to 10. For both observers, the rating of beauty increased from roughly 3.5 to 6 as the field of view grew from 6° to 210°. The increase, about 2.5 points, is large, corresponding roughly to the difference between ratings of a favourite and an ordinary painting. Note that the horizontal scale has logarithmic spacing. Beauty goes up about 1.5 points as the view is increased from 6° to 56° and increases another point as the view is increased to 210°. The results show that restricting the observers' peripheral vision reduced the viewing pleasure. Since, with Santayana, beauty is pleasure, restricting the field reduced the beauty of the landscape for these two observers of the New Jersey skyline.

Of course, the sensory experiences that landscape provides – from scents to sounds to ranges of temperature to changes in weather – cannot be rendered on a two-dimensional surface. Or can they? Japanese prints and paintings have captured vivid scenes of windy days, of rain, and of snow. Using poetic language, haikus have also created such images. In contemporary work, only Ian Hamilton Finlay has achieved the seamless integration of words into landscape, though there are many 18th-century examples of it, which Finlay himself cites in his own

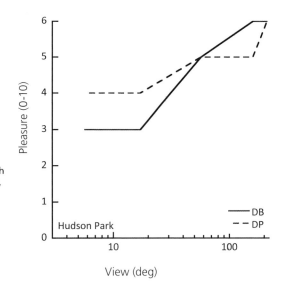

Diana Balmori and Denis Pelli, how beauty grows with scope of view, 23 April 2010, New York City, New York, USA. Graph.
Measurements taken by reducing peripheral vision were recorded in Manhattan's Hudson River Park at 14th Street at 3.30pm with participants facing west.

work.[2] The words are part of his landscape. They are also part of small books he designs in which words are composed spatially on the page, similar to concrete poetry, as in this example resembling a waterfall:[3]

Cascade

The one
water

sings its
separate

small
pop songs

as it
falls

The work of landscape representation is also affected by its intended audience. Unlike architecture, landscape is imperfectly understood by the general public, who sometimes confuse it with horticulture or with ecology or think of it as a green mantle surrounding buildings. Olmsted is often the only name that people associate with large open-air designed landscapes over the last century, though this is rapidly changing. Still, public understanding of the discipline lags behind that of architecture. Representation then

becomes even more burdened with recognition, and since three-dimensional built models are not effective for rendering landscape (as they are for architecture), communicating detailed design becomes even more difficult, demanding a level of realism that defeats many designers' aims. It is tempting to quote Raphael who dismisses perspective as the tool of painters, and unnecessary for the architect, being just a seductive feature for those who do not understand other forms of architectural drawing.[4]

The examples of contemporary work that follow can be better understood and appreciated in light of this brief overview of some of the difficulties involved in landscape representation.

Landscape Urbanism

After 1911, when all the arts broke away from the past, new movements – such as Surrealism, Constructivism, Cubism, Futurism, Dadaism and Expressionism – arose. In contrast, the individuals whose work is discussed later in this chapter have deliberately chosen not to be part of any movement. But there is a group of practitioners who have developed an overarching concept, Landscape Urbanism, for a new approach to the reinvented discipline of landscape architecture, addressing its change of scale and the shift to working in an urban context. Therefore, although Landscape Urbanism has been interpreted and reinterpreted by different people within the group, and although initially

(Opposite left) Wallace, McHarg, Roberts & Todd, urbanisation areas, Staten Island, New York City, New York, USA, 1968. Photograph of a map study.
McHarg pioneered the use of map overlays, where physiographic features were isolated and then superimposed. In this image from a study for Richmond Parkway, McHarg and his colleagues studied the density of urbanisation.

(Opposite right) Wallace, McHarg, Roberts & Todd, conservation, recreation and urbanisation areas, Staten Island, New York City, New York, USA, 1968. Photograph of a map study.
The hybrid image shown here overlays various maps, presenting a proposed route for a controversial five-mile stretch of Staten Island's Richmond Parkway by exploring ecological, recreational and urban interests. Analyses like this were used to select a path for the Parkway that would have least impact on residents.

URBANIZATION AREAS

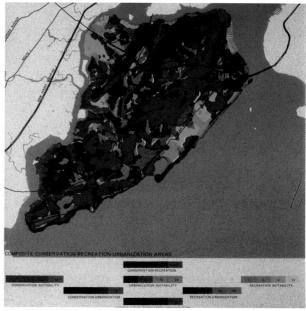

COMPOSITE CONSERVATION RECREATION URBANIZATION AREAS

my intent was to deal only with specific individuals and issues of landscape representation in their work, because a movement which has favoured a particular form of representation has emerged there is a good case for addressing Landscape Urbanism in terms of representation as a group philosophy. The disciplines it is conceptually closest to are urban design and especially ecology. Two founding practitioners are highlighted – Charles Waldheim and James Corner

– to give a better sense of Landscape Urbanism as a movement and its central ideas.

Charles Waldheim was the movement's founder. Trained as an architect, he turned to landscape design and is at present chair of the Department of Landscape Architecture at Harvard University. In *The Landscape Urbanism Reader*, which he edited, he writes this 'book records the subtle shifts and sharp shocks of a deep, ongoing, disciplinary breakdown, in favor of a new object, a new language'.[5] The 14 thoughtful essays by others address the nature of the changes in social and economic conditions and the resulting issues of representation, although those issues are not their focus.

The disciplinary breakdown is very real, as is the search for a new language, which Landscape Urbanism has been actively seeking. Those developments arguably have their roots in Ian McHarg's earlier work, with its focus on mapping and creating diagrams of ecological processes, and in particular in its effective analogue overlapping of maps. That method was adopted later in digital GIS (Geographic Information System) technology, though with a different emphasis. McHarg's use of transparent map overlays puts dissimilar, transdisciplinary layers in stacks, starting at the bottom with natural processes and ending at the top with social and cultural ones. However, although it was McHarg who made ecology the basis of urban planning, he ignored the artistic values of landscape. In a way, he set those values aside. Digitalisation has further contributed to the lack of aesthetics in map layering and has also resulted in the intensification of the focus on process over product. It is not so much that our tools dictate our behaviour, but rather that they subtly influence it unless we ensure that no matter which tools we use, our intention prevails in our work.

Corner is the most important practitioner among the contributors to *The Landscape Urbanism Reader*. Born in England, with a master's degree in landscape architecture from the University of Pennsylvania, which he eventually chaired from 2000 through 2012, his practice, Field Operations, is based in Philadelphia and New York. In his essay, 'Terra Fluxus', he describes the intellectual underpinnings of the Landscape Urbanist agenda, which is rooted in the historical development of architecture, urban design and urban planning as disciplines.[6] He specifies four elements on which the emerging Landscape Urbanist practice is based: ecological and urban processes over time, the staging of horizontal surfaces, the operational method and the role of imagination. Along with many others in the Landscape Urbanism movement, he sees the need for an inventive reorganisation of its two underlying disciplines in order to deal with the restructuring of the contemporary city, which is a continuous process.

Landscape Urbanism's contribution to forms of representation lies in the importance it gives to the diagram as well as to mapping. The diagram's first point of reference is architecture; ecology is its second. Mapping's springboard is urban planning. Diagrams and mapping are Landscape Urbanism's basic tools for representation, lining up landscape with architectural and urban practices.

Corner has identified three difficulties of landscape representation: '(1) the designer's indirect and detached or remote access to the landscape

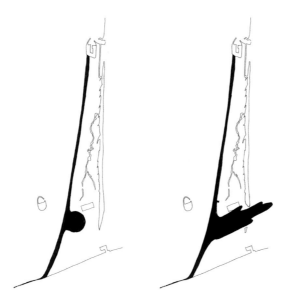

West 8, diagrams of landscape and dune evolution, Duindoornstad, Rotterdam, the Netherlands, 1995. Digital diagram.
These diagrams and time sequence studies examine how dunes are formed and affected by wind, water and vegetation.

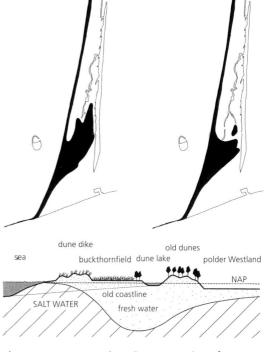

medium; (2) the incongruity of drawing with respect to its subject – its abstractness with respect to actual landscape experience; and (3) the anterior, prevenient function of the drawing – its generative role. Paradoxically it is these three same characteristics that make such drawing enigmatic in both a negative and positive sense.'[7]

Among Landscape Urbanists, the conceptual weight of the project is now focused on diagrams, which are used to show biological, ecological and urban processes over time. Representation of process is the central concern of Landscape Urbanism; the movement's view of nature as process guides the designers in developing their designs.

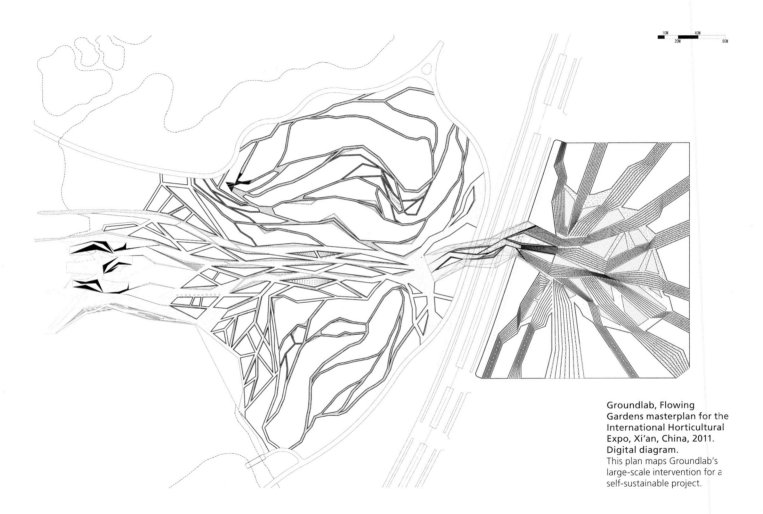

Groundlab, Flowing
Gardens masterplan for the
International Horticultural
Expo, Xi'an, China, 2011.
Digital diagram.
This plan maps Groundlab's
large-scale intervention for a
self-sustainable project.

Waldheim considers the diagrams generated by OMA/Rem Koolhaas and the ones created by Bernard Tschumi for the 1983 Parc de La Villette competition to be paradigmatic. This points to Landscape Urbanism's close connection to architecture, though it indicates a changed relationship between the disciplines, with landscape taking the lead. Corner's diagrams for the Toronto and Fresh Kills competitions, illustrated overleaf, are also considered archetypal for Landscape Urbanism; process is clearly addressed in both of them. And in West 8's diagram for Duindoornstad, a new coastal city near Rotterdam, a time sequence illustrates process, from the creation of two artificial islands to the raising of the coastal zone and the formation of a duneland that evolves according to effects of wind, water and vegetation – recalling McHarg's studies of the evolution of dunes. Adriaan Geuze writes that the design 'is continually evolving based as it is on civil-engineering and landscape identities' rather than being 'designed with an end result in mind'.[8]

As significant as the diagram, and in a way tied to it, is the attention and concentration on horizontal surfaces, that

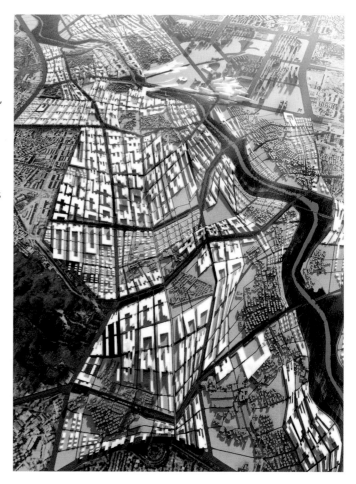

Groundlab, Deep Ground, Longgang masterplan aerial view, Shenzhen, China, 2008. Digital rendering.
In this project, Groundlab worked at the scale of a city to deal with the contemporary challenges of modern China: through the concept of 'thickened ground', multiple ground data are fused to foster orientation and connectivity.

is, modelling with thematic layers. A continuation of McHarg's approach, cartographic modelling and mapping in general have risen again in importance after mapping's near demise following the decimation of geography departments at universities across the country in the 1960s. The combination of mapping, aerial photography and computation, reinforced by data from Google Earth, has made cartographic modelling an indispensable tool. In addition, because it is oriented more towards process than product,

cartographic modelling is very well suited to the representation of Landscape Urbanism design; the change in the scale of landscape projects, which now often cover vast areas, has undoubtedly contributed to the importance of cartographic modelling as well. Groundlab's design on the horizontal plane of the masterplan for a horticultural expo in China in 2011 and their aerial view of the masterplan for Longgang, Shenzhen, show two aspects of this use of mapping. Kate Orff's recent analysis of the petrochemical

Kate Orff, Petrochemical America, map locating the industries of River Road and their primary chemical and material outputs, 2012. Digital diagram.
Orff's investigation into America's energy landscape, Petrochemical America (Aperture Foundation, 2012), uses mapping strategies to analyse the sites, processes, cycles and effects of America's energy-consumption patterns.

industry along a section of the southern United States is basically a mapping and photographic study, which demonstrates how mapping can be used to deal with large geographic areas.

Field Operations' Fresh Kills Park project consists of the transformation of a major waste dump on Staten Island, New York, into a public park. The layered diagrammatic mapping of the site's surface begins with the wetland that existed below it before 1948, when it was converted to a city dump. Next comes the accumulation and distribution of tons of waste; a plan for collecting and containing liquids; a methane gas extraction network; the placement of an impermeable liner and soil cover; a system for directing surface water movement; and finally, the top three layers: the new habitat, new circulation and new programmes. Also consider, for example, the diagrams of grassland and woodland development and their sequential location over a 40-year period that are also part of the Fresh Kills Park project. They describe the evolution and cultivation of habitats over time and locate them in the order that they will occur.

Corner's diagram of emergence through adaptive management for Downsview Park in Toronto charts different biotopes in a large, complex urban area from initial propagation through to self-organisation and adaptation over a five-year period. It also enables us to see ecological and biological processes under human management as they develop over time.

Field Operations, Fresh Kills Park, Staten Island, New York City, New York, USA, 2004. Digital diagram showing layers of Fresh Kills lifescape.
Fresh Kills on Staten Island functioned as landfill for New York City for over 50 years. This diagram works diachronically to show Field Operations' long-term strategies of agricultural processes and natural practices as a means of rehabilitating Fresh Kills.

NEW PROGRAMME

NEW CIRCULATION

NEW HABITAT

soil cover

surface water

impermeable liner

gas extraction network

liquid collection and containment

160 million tons of waste

wetland prior to 1948

2001   **2002**   **2003**

SITE HYDROLOGY: 100% ON-SITE SELF SUSTAINABLE WATER BALANCE BY YEAR ONE

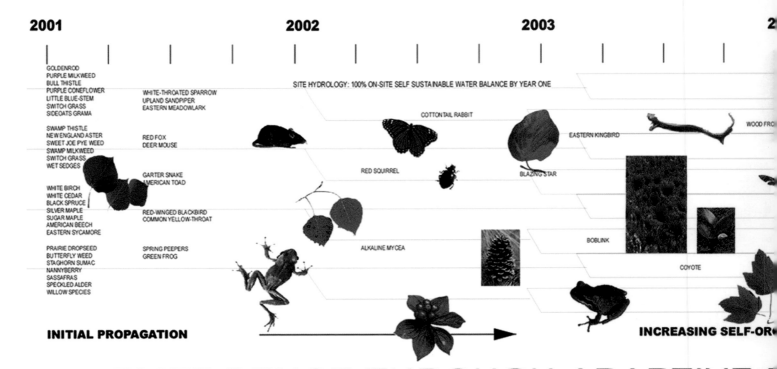

GOLDENROD
PURPLE MILKWEED
BULL THISTLE
PURPLE CONEFLOWER
LITTLE BLUE-STEM
SWITCH GRASS
SIDEOATS GRAMA

WHITE-THROATED SPARROW
UPLAND SANDPIPER
EASTERN MEADOWLARK

SWAMP THISTLE
NEW ENGLAND ASTER
SWEET JOE PYE WEED
SWAMP MILKWEED
SWITCH GRASS
WET SEDGES

RED FOX
DEER MOUSE

WHITE BIRCH
WHITE CEDAR
BLACK SPRUCE
SILVER MAPLE
SUGAR MAPLE
AMERICAN BEECH
EASTERN SYCAMORE

GARTER SNAKE
AMERICAN TOAD

RED-WINGED BLACKBIRD
COMMON YELLOW-THROAT

PRAIRIE DROPSEED
BUTTERFLY WEED
STAGHORN SUMAC
NANNYBERRY
SASSAFRAS
SPECKLED ALDER
WILLOW SPECIES

SPRING PEEPERS
GREEN FROG

COTTONTAIL RABBIT

RED SQUIRREL

ALKALINE MYCEA

EASTERN KINGBIRD

BLAZING STAR

BOBLINK

COYOTE

WOOD FRO

WOOD FRO

INITIAL PROPAGATION

INCREASING SELF-ORG

EMERGENCE THROUGH ADAPTIVE

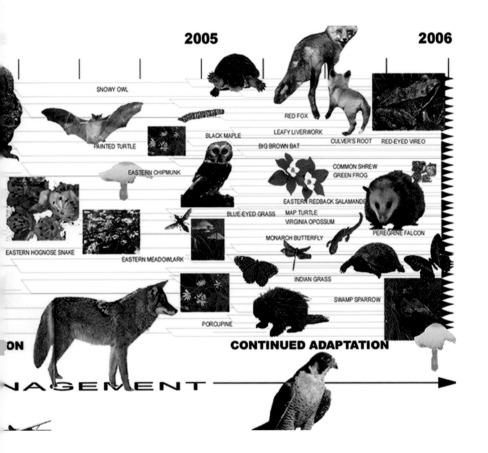

2005   2006

SNOWY OWL

RED FOX

PAINTED TURTLE

BLACK MAPLE

LEAFY LIVERWORK

BIG BROWN BAT

CULVER'S ROOT   RED-EYED VIREO

EASTERN CHIPMUNK

COMMON SHREW

GREEN FROG

EASTERN REDBACK SALAMANDER

BLUE-EYED GRASS MAP TURTLE

VIRGINIA OPOSSUM

PEREGRINE FALCON

MONARCH BUTTERFLY

EASTERN HOGNOSE SNAKE

EASTERN MEADOWLARK

INDIAN GRASS

SWAMP SPARROW

PORCUPINE

CONTINUED ADAPTATION

ON

NAGEMENT

To summarise, in Landscape Urbanism, the study of the horizontal plane used as a strategy in mapping gives horizontality a predominant role not just in representation but also in design and – as the movement's name implies – clearly ties Landscape Urbanism to urban planning. The second important element of Landscape Urbanism's representation, the diagram, addresses biological and ecological processes, thereby introducing the element of time – which has until now been ignored by landscape architecture on the whole – into representation in a much more deliberate way.

Bernard Lassus

Nothing can offer a starker contrast to the approach of Landscape Urbanism's forms of representation than the work of Bernard Lassus, who completely rejects creating a representation of a landscape. When asked about how and in what medium he would represent his project at Crazannes (an abandoned quarry by a highway), he replied, 'Rent a car and drive down to Crazannes. The only thing that is not misleading,' he added, 'is what is on the ground.' When considering Lassus's work, it is relevant to know that he studied with Fernand Léger at the Ecole des Beaux-Arts, that he was a French kinetic artist and shifted to landscape work in the late '60s, that he is a phenomenological artist influenced by Maurice Merleau-Ponty, and that he is particularly interested in connections that humans have with the rest of nature through their senses. His background in working under Léger, with whom he shared an interest in breaking away from the limits of the pictorial frame, shows both the continuity and the transformation of important ideas in landscape, and the surviving connection between painting and landscape. Lassus's rupture with the previous traditions of landscape practice is tangible, but even when a practitioner has been able to change historical landscape concepts to fit new needs, long-embedded ideas re-emerge – if only as references.

Lassus's Crazannes design emerged from a motorway project that went through a limestone pit where stone had been quarried for gravel beginning under the Romans in the 2nd century AD and continuing through to 1960. The work on the motorway uncovered this long story of human exploitation of nature. When the project leader learned that an ancient quarry had been found at the site, he decided that it should be preserved.

Lassus worked on the landscape not through drawings but with bulldozers. He and the bulldozer crew scraped the face of the quarry rather than dynamiting it, sculpting two sides of a road. When the client insisted they needed a drawing of the project to show to the public, Lassus photographed the whole

length of the limestone face and then made a drawing above it, after the fact. The client liked the drawing, but still wanted to know what Lassus would construct at the site. Lassus spent a summer drawing artificial rocks that he would eventually make into constructed pieces for the site. He built one and made a plan for seven more. Then he said, 'the project is finished, it is a two-minute-long landscape'. He spoke of it having a rhythm, like jazz. The strong contrast between the yellow limestone and the dark holes, like black grottoes, was what created the rhythm, which is the most important part of the experience of Crazannes and an abstraction of it.

The road itself was not a landscape; the motorway was just a convenience. The traveller realises at a glance that there is something interesting there, a background becoming foreground. A drawing cannot portray what you experience travelling at 30 metres per second. Lassus wanted Crazannes to be a visual experience of travel and of the discovery of human beings' presence in the quarry and the ruins they left behind, rather than the quarry simply being something to look at. He re-establishes the former presence of humans in nature and makes something new from it, while pulling you away from the highway to the landscape through successive side views.

Lassus's garden for the Colas Group, situated about 10 miles (16 kilometres) from Versailles, takes the issue of representation to a higher and more abstract

(Previous page) Field Operations, Downsview Park, Toronto, Ontario, Canada, 2000. Digital diagram.
Field Operations' competition entry diagram shows how new animal and plant species would emerge through adaptive management at the site.

Bernard Lassus, rock formations sketch – rest area of Crazannes – motorway A837, France, 1993–8. Pen on paper.
For the Crazannes quarries project, both sides of a rock face bordering a French motorway were excavated, sculpted and transformed to create a design that would draw passing motorists.

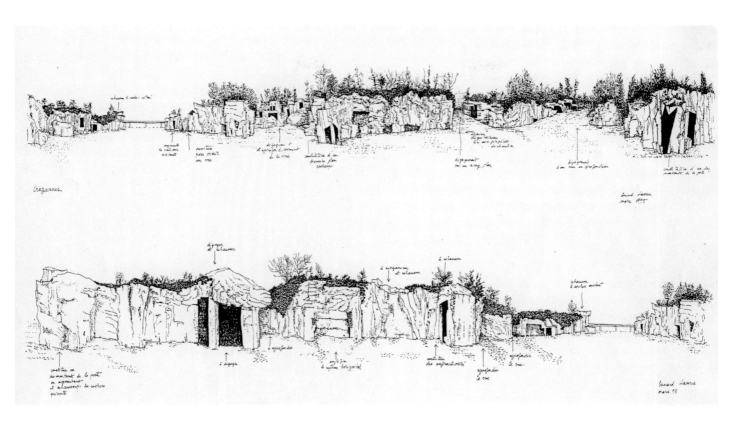

level. After stating that he is against representation, that is representing his landscape design in a drawing, Lassus here uses the designed and built landscape itself as a representation. For the garden itself is a representation of features of Versailles. Colas has a curious mixture of actual vegetation and metal representations of vegetation. In the historic section of this book, I discuss the representation of representation which occurred in French garden theatres, where stage vegetation and the real garden playfully intermingled; simulacra of vegetation were placed in the garden, and real vegetation was put in the theatre, offering a view of a central path that was part theatrical stage set and part real garden. There are echoes of this at Colas in the view down the Salle Verte in a bosquet of the Petit Parc. But Lassus pushed the connection: at Colas the whole three-dimensional, real garden is a representation, or rather, a representation of a representation. By using representations of real plants, Lassus ensures that Colas is understood as a representation. And it is not temporary stage scenery, but a garden.

His waterfall made out of red light tubes and the artificial grotto in which it stands are examples of the interplay of the parts of the garden, for which he made many studies. Lassus wanted a waterfall at Colas, but did not want to make an actual waterfall; he insisted on a representation of one instead. The concept for the garden was explained to the client, but no presentation drawings were made; the client trusted Lassus and did not ask for them. Lassus did make study sketches, including drawings of the grotto, waterfall and other early sketches, but they were meant as personal explorations. The only representation prepared for the public consisted of photographs of the built garden.

In Colas, Lassus was extremely interested in the garden's visual properties of parts; six months

Bernard Lassus, fountain of light sketch, Théâtre de Verdure, Les Jardins Suspendus de Colas, Boulogne-Billancourt, France, 2006. Pen on paper. The Colas Garden – Le Jardin du Jeu des Saisons, Le Jardin de Pins, Le Jardin de l'Attente, Le Théâtre de Verdure (2000–07) – is a series of roof gardens created for the headquarters of the Colas Corporation.

Bernard Lassus, grotto
sketch, Théâtre de Verdure,
Les Jardins Suspendus de
Colas, Boulogne-Billancourt,
France, 2006. Crayon on
paper.
This sketch of a grotto – an
historically important element
of gardens that was meant to
look as if made by nature – was
illuminated in bright red to
stress its artificiality.

Cascade et rochers

Sept 06

(Opposite) Bernard Lassus, grotto and fountain of light, Théâtre de Verdure, Les Jardins Suspendus de Colas, Boulogne-Billancourt, France, 2007. Photograph. Lassus combines actual vegetation and metal representations of vegetation to highlight the constructive act of making gardens.

Bernard Lassus, early sketch for Le Jardin du Jeu des Saisons, Colas, Boulogne-Billancourt, France, 2001–2. This is Lassus's earliest sketch for the lower terrace of Le Jardin du Jeu des Saisons. The Jardin du Jeu des Saisons is composed of four gardens that contain sets of metal trees or shrubs, each painted a different colour to represent a season.

were spent studying the garden's colours, for example. Lassus made artificial trees for the four seasons, which the client could change according to the time of year. The flowers in the garden are constructed; they hover between abstraction and representation. Lassus has purposely crossed the historical chasm between the artificial and the natural, which has been the bane of landscape architects since the 20th century, when 'artificial' ceased to be meaningful. And at the same time, he has enlarged the meaning of representation.

Lassus understands landscape as a process in the viewer's mind, creating a fleeting moment of integration. Michel Conan has said of Lassus's interpretation of landscape, 'He takes nature to be the outcome of human interaction with the world as it evolves through time, where the distinction between artificial and natural is only a convention, if not a passing illusion.'[9]

inquiry. If the present formal break with the past has any antecedents (which is hard to assess, since the current situation is a new one), it is in those years. Johanson's move into landscape design, which began when the magazine *House & Garden* asked her to design a garden from an artist's perspective, led her to explore landscape through the 147 gardens she drew for them. She never returned to painting per se after that.

It is also worth noting that Johanson

Patricia Johanson

When Patricia Johanson, who was seen as a young up-and-coming artist, started to distance herself from painting in 1969, landscape as a discipline had arrived at another turning point. That was the year McHarg's *Design with Nature* was published.[10] A movement in sculpture called Earthworks (after the fact, as with most art movements) also began around the same time, as environmentalism and ecology emerged as fields of

began her career as a minimalist painter. An American artist born in New York City and a painting major at Bennington College, she is a pioneer in the field of eco-art (1969). In her landscape designs, plants or creatures on the site are represented as formal, realistically rendered mythical figures. Landscape became Johanson's vehicle for investigating the new view of nature in which humans are an integral part, and she made that her artistic endeavour. Her designs aim to

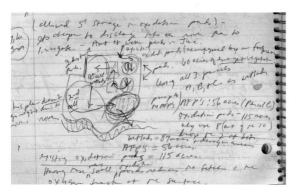

Patricia Johanson, lined notebook sketch for Ellis Creek Water Recycling Facility, Petaluma, California, USA, 2003. Ballpoint pen on paper.
Johanson describes her initial sketches as 'hen scratchings', later translated into working drawings by engineers.

establish relationships between people and water, soil, plants, insects, birds, mammals and everything else in nature. Her work is not ecology, but it works ecologically. Nor is her work didactic; instead, she frames nature in a way that makes it speak about how it can best function to enhance the lives of those in it.

In Johanson's work, the notebook plays a crucial role. It is where her ideas are jotted down and then developed. You can see the visible marks of her thinking there and follow the evolution of an idea. As the ideas develop, they integrate into drawings and take on vivid colours.

If you ask her about her first sketches, she will answer immediately, mentioning the 'hen scratchings' she makes when she starts to put ideas down. But when you ask about final drawings, she will say, 'but that is not how I work'. Instead, she works by developing those

first sketches, making them more and more detailed and covering them with notes. At each stage, to make sure that the civil engineers on her project understand what she is after, she discusses the drawings with them. 'They always want to neaten up my drawings,' she says. After the engineers' revisions, she returns to the drawings, adding another layer as the work proceeds. She will not show the drawings to the clients, but she will explain her work, telling them about her ideas and about her process with the engineers.

Johanson studied architecture and civil engineering after the *House & Garden* commission, and therefore, though at first glance her drawings appear loose, they are in fact to scale in all their details. The significance of her work lies in this quite original mixture of artistic expression, ecology and civil engineering – a difficult and very original path that breaks down the rather narrow definition of landscape as a discipline.

When you visit the site of the Ellis Creek Water Recycling Facility in Petaluma, California, you encounter a riddle. White mice live in this area and are an endangered protected species. The animal is encoded as a figure in the design, but it is not visible at ground level, although it is a link to the whole system.

Johanson creates these images to stimulate the public's interest in the relation of humans to the rest of nature. The images have a symbolic presence. There are signs referring to them and to the what

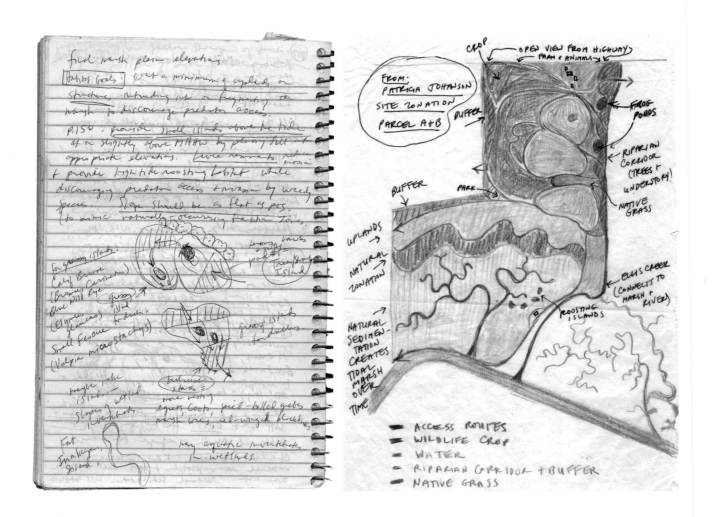

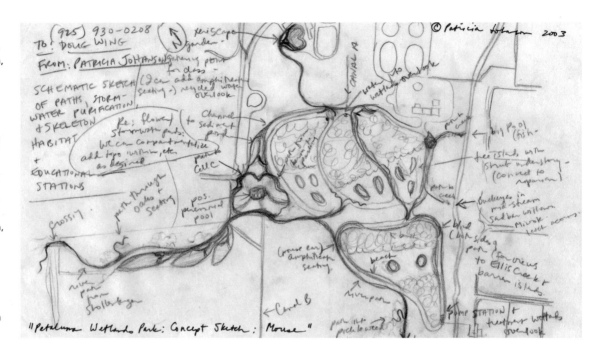

(Opposite left) Patricia Johanson, lined notebook sketch for Ellis Creek Water Recycling Facility, Petaluma, California, USA, 2003. Ballpoint pen on paper.
This initial sketch shows Johanson's first ideas about how to tackle the problem of water circulation through the polishing wetlands in the area adjacent to Lakeville Highway and a nearby business park in Petaluma, California.

(Opposite right) Patricia Johanson, butterfly zones sketch, Ellis Creek Water Recycling Facility, Petaluma, California, USA, 2002. Coloured pencil on paper.
This butterfly zones sketch shows three polishing ponds surrounded by agricultural fields (top) with the Petaluma River and tidal wetlands (bottom). The butterfly design was one of three designs for the project.

Patricia Johanson, working drawing, Ellis Creek Water Recycling Facility, Petaluma, California, USA, 2003. Pencil and ink on vellum.
This is an initial sketch for what would become the Mouse's nose and the Morning Glory pools.

and why of their being there. Thus, through the site as well as through her notebooks, your experience of the design intensifies. Every aspect of nature there becomes an actor in the work. Of the sketch for the California project, she says, 'In this drawing, I would be talking about the sewage processing through the zoned (densely vegetated and open water) areas of the ponds; the islands that channel the flow; and the

water transfer structures (water flows by gravity from the three parallel ponds down to the Mouse's nose). Also, the storm water processing through the Morning Glory, coming off Lakeville Highway (at the top) and the business park at left does look a bit like art because I always color everything, but the design is deeply functional and carefully choreographed. If you look at the earliest sketches, you'll see that the changes have to do with process (the treatment train – how the water circulates, where it enters, and where it ends up), and this was the most elegant solution.'[11]

As to later, more finished drawings that she passes on to the engineers (such as that of the Mouse shown overleaf), she says, 'I guess this would be an example, with my hen scratchings made a bit neater by the engineers, and my site plan printed with text that someone can actually read. The professional members of the team always try to make my work look more presentable, but my drawings are all to scale, so they do not make changes.'[12] Johanson wants her drawings to be technical and efficient, but she wants the design to lead to the development of life, the life of those living in it.

The technical side of the project is shaped mainly through engineering. So she continually engages in a dialogue with the engineers to ensure that the designs do not become merely economically driven, technical pursuits and that the engineers will include the logic of life and the process of enriching biotopes in their subsequent work. Johanson considers what animals live on the site, what kind of food they have, and how to provide for the fish so they will remain on the site. She started out with a very technical programme for the project. The two islands became the eyes of the Mouse, which were essential to the water treatment process. As a result, they were accepted by the engineers, who otherwise tended to remove the forms Johanson introduced.

The whole design became a symbol of the protection of the marsh, and Johanson skilfully convinced the client and the engineers about the barely visible forms of life there and the need to safeguard them. Moreover, she simultaneously made the water treatment functions the technical working model for the site. In her detailed study of Johanson's work, Xin Wu has explained that Johanson's art is not about form: 'The shapes and colors she introduces in the design are mere props to guide visitors to discover natural wonders that would be ignored otherwise'.[13]

By these means, Johanson created an enhanced natural environment that attracts the public. She rejoiced in the family of otters who invited themselves to the islands, but the local bird-lovers' association wanted to get rid of them and forbade people from going to the marsh. There is no easy solution when different groups single out different species for preferential treatment. It represents one of the many debates taking place in landscape architecture, which is in turn becoming the source of a new conversation about the dynamics of nature and about human beings – who finally recognise that they too are part of nature – as important agents within it. Landscape now sits in the crossfire of this argument, in which human behaviour towards other species is keenly disputed. Johanson's project is a good example of this, and it is one in which she made a clear stand for the otters.

Johanson understands the landscape as energy,

(Opposite left) Patricia Johanson, Mouse sketch, Ellis Creek Water Recycling Facility, Petaluma, California, USA, 2007. Coloured pencil and ink on printed plan. This drawing exists in many prior iterations of an earlier date, but this particular version – additional colouring on a printed plan – was made to show the location of the interpretive signage, which was required by the California Coastal Conservancy. Johanson writes that she colours her drawings with a deeply 'choreographed' structure in mind. Here, three blue ponds collect water that drains by gravitational force to the 'Mouse's nose' represented at the lower right in green and blue.

(Opposite right) Patricia Johanson, Morning Glory pools sketch, Ellis Creek Water Recycling Facility, Petaluma, California, USA, 2004. Acrylic, ink, pastel and coloured pencil on vellum. While Johanson generates the design, she does not create final renderings.

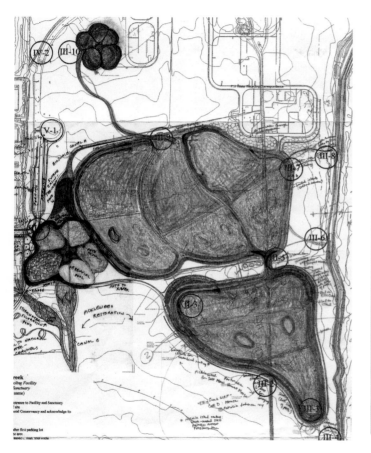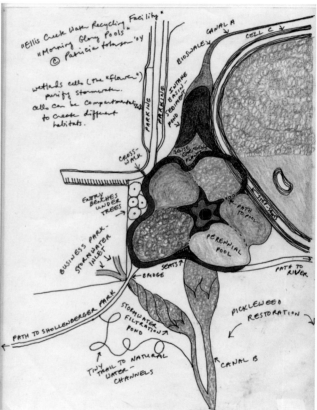

movement and duration, to paraphrase Henri Bergson. These are three things which humans can gain from engaging with landscape. And she is the hermeneutist translating through artistic language that engagement.

Richard Haag (Rich Haag Associates)

An example of work that does not lend itself to being represented in drawings, except in early sketches, is that of the American landscape architect Richard Haag. His practice is based in Seattle, Washington, and all his projects are in the north-western United States. Haag created the Department of Landscape Architecture at the University of Washington and his ecological and minimalist approach has influenced a generation of landscape designers in the north-west. Looking at his work helps us to understand what kinds of landscape designs can or cannot be communicated through drawings.

Haag primarily works on-site. His Gas Works Park in Seattle can be seen as a representation of what the site really is: an abandoned industrial plant and its grounds, made into public space that is not prettified or parkified. The project preceded by many years Peter Latz's better-known Duisburg-Nord Landscape Park in Germany where preserved industrial ruins are the bases for his park. The main drawing of Gas Works is a technical hardline plan, which is a guide for the construction of the landscape and is not meant to represent the project to the client or the public, while Haag's rough early sketch for Gas Works captures both its simplicity and (like all early sketches) an idea for the project. He retained spare unadorned remains of the old machinery and whichever ancillary buildings could be used. Accepting them as they were, emanating raw power, he declared that they were part of the site and should be included in the public space, so inviting visitors to look at them. If a climber hadn't had an accident on the chimneys in the early days of Gas Works, these would have remained open for people to explore, which is what Haag wanted, and still wants. The only thing that he added to the site was a large earth mound that he converted into a lookout.

Many people misinterpret Gas Works Park. Some see it as a historical or industrial preservation project, but Haag's real intent was to make visible the beauty of the Gas Works plant and then find ways of cleaning up the soil that had been polluted by the industry there, which he succeeded in doing. He likes what the Gas Works plant represented, but does not romanticise it. I asked him if he was trying to say that it was a picture of the passing of a culture's power, and he said, 'I can use that'.

There are no final great renderings of Haag's landscapes. However, he creates early sketches in which he puts his ideas for a landscape down on paper, and those drawings align with his work. The rest of it is done at the site, where he adds modestly

Richard Haag, The Big Moves, Gas Works Park, Seattle, Washington, USA, 1971. Pencil on paper. Though local officials wanted to tear down the industrial buildings of a former plant on the site, Haag convinced them to keep a significant part for Gas Works Park (1971–88), located on Lake Union in Seattle. This is an early sketch for the project has varying line weights. Gas Works Park is now listed on the National Register of Historic Places.

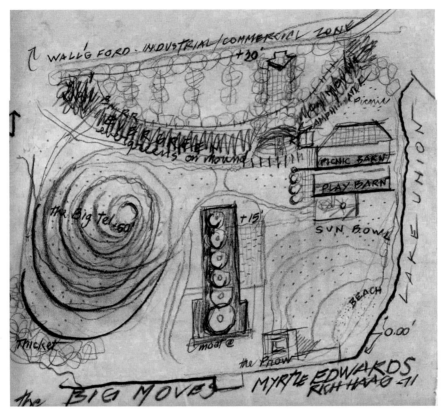

qualities and allows us to see what is there; you could argue that his work on the ground is a representation of the actual site. For example, the pool garden at the Bloedel Reserve on Bainbridge Island, off the shore of Seattle, was put there by Bloedel with the guidance of a landscape architect who worked on the site prior to Haag's involvement. Haag only added the hedge around the pool. It was enough. It is the sort of thing Haag does extremely well. Elsewhere at Bloedel he drew attention to a forest and to moss; in another garden there, he shaped a small central area with intersecting inclined planes.

Photographing the site both before Haag works on it, and then again after his modest interventions,

to what is there or removes a moderate amount from it. The result of these subtle changes is that the landscape becomes visible. Haag intensifies its existing

best represents this kind of work. Photographs of the four gardens at Bloedel Reserve convey little of what Haag did because they do not show what the site was like prior to his working there. His early sketches for Bloedel reflect the simplicity of the design, representing the gardens diagrammatically.

Haag sees nature as the power to make human endeavours into ruins, and he has been compared to the Dutch artist Louis-Guillaume Le Roy and the Belgian architect Lucien Kroll, two figures of the Situationist International.[14]

Swimming Pool transformed into a Moss Sculpture Garden set into a plane of MOSS & surrounded by mountains for the plain — The 'GARDEN of PLANES' BLOEDEL RESERVE DESIGNER: RICHARD HAAG - 7-20-81

(Opposite top) **Richard Haag, Reflection Garden, Bloedel Reserve, Bainbridge Island, Puget Sound, Washington, USA, 1979–84. Photograph.**
Named after its former timber-baron owner, Bloedel Reserve is composed of a series of landscape events and places in an area that had been clear-cut at the start of the 20th century. The Reflection Garden is framed by 12-foot (3.65-metre) high clipped yew hedges around a pool reflecting the surrounding tall trees.

(Opposite below) **Richard Haag, Reflection Garden, Bloedel Reserve, Bainbridge Island, Puget Sound, Washington, USA, 1979–84. Mixed media.**
The plan of the Reflection Garden reveals its formal rectilinearity of both basin and hedge juxtaposed against the neighbouring paths and gardens.

Richard Haag, The Garden of Planes, Bloedel Reserve, Bainbridge Island, Puget Sound, Washington, USA, 1981. Pencil on vellum.
Haag inscribed this sheet with the description, 'Swimming pool transformed into a moss sculpture garden set into a plane/plain of moss and surrounded by mountains for the Bloedel Reserve.'

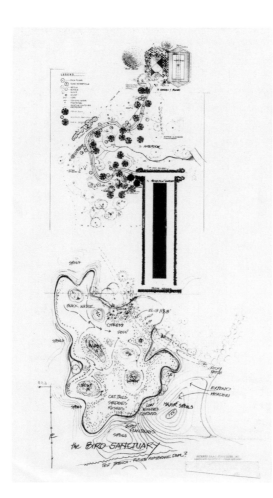

Stig L Andersson (SLA)

I derive great pleasure from the work of Stig Andersson and the representation of it. He appeals to the senses and has found a way of conveying the things he finds delightful. He stands out for his ability to make his work in cities seem like a paean to the presence of nature there, though he makes it clear that nature is separate and distinct from his designed landscape. Danish by birth, he is creative director of his practice, SLA, based in Copenhagen. His was the first office to receive the European Landscape Award from the international landscape architecture magazine *Topos*, precisely for his focus on sensory urban spaces.

For Andersson, a city's nature is in the sun shining down on it, in the rain, in the puddles reflecting the sky after a storm, in birdsong, in the murmur of water, in the wind smelling of the sea. He sees his task as one of drawing attention to common everyday smells, sights, sounds and textures of nature that are very much part of the city but that usually go unnoticed. He doesn't bring parks or plantings into the city to help us experience nature there. Instead, by provoking the senses, he directs us to notice what is already around us. He places a greater emphasis on the tactile and the aural than on the visual. His design is a frame that reveals the presence of these elements. In an early sketch for the Charlotte Garden in Copenhagen, he introduced a parterre with puddles of water and an alleyway paved with seashells that crackle underfoot.

Each of these is made to awaken us for a moment to our surroundings, forcing us to be aware of them.

This attempt to create a sensory connectivity is expressed in Andersson's drawings, particularly in his very early sketches, which are often done in loose watercolour strokes that have a fresh childlike quality. How do you convey landscapes designed more for the touch than for the eye? In the Mud Garden in Xi'an, China, that Andersson designed for an annual expo of 2011, he does just that. It delights in the reddish mud that local residents consider more of an inconvenience than an asset. His early sketches refer to the landscape's materials – water, snow, rain, mud. The mud becomes sculptures that are baked and then painted fiery red, intensifying the colour of the soil to make it clear that these are artificial constructions. He reinvents Chinese garden rocks, and in the process, draws attention to the earth he uses to create them. There is a large yellow bridge across a major river not too far from the site. In the spirit of the familiar Chinese and Japanese

Stig Andersson with Stig's daughter Xenia, first sketch, Yellow Mud Garden, Xi'an International Horticultural Expo, China, 2010. Marker on notebook paper.
Andersson took initial inspiration for his Yellow Mud Garden from drawings made with his daughter, Xenia.

Stig Andersson, first sketch, Yellow Mud Garden, Xi'an International Horticultural Expo, China, 2010. Marker on paper.
This sketch shows Andersson's interest in the materials of water, snow and rain. Abstract sculptural forms allude to Chinese garden rocks and the reddish soil commonly found in Xi'an and celebrated in the garden.

Stig Andersson, Yellow Mud Garden, Xi'an International Horticultural Expo, China, 2011. Photograph.
The 1,000-square-metre (10,800-square-foot) garden was SLA's 2010–11 contribution to the Xi'an international landscape exhibition. SLA was one of eight teams specially invited to participate in the exhibition.

landscape aesthetic, Andersson builds a bridge across the garden's shallow waters and mud fields and paints it yellow, as if he were miniaturising aspects of the surrounding landscape.

Andersson's presentation drawings look to the tradition of Chinese landscape drawings and are mixed with photographic images of real plants – an unlikely combination that succeeds in this case. They are accompanied by a plan showing all the parts of the garden in different colours. It is a schematic plan, yet it and the elevation for the garden are treated as paintings and rendered in vivid hues. We have here a renewal of landscape's connection to painting.

In Andersson's own words: 'The special thing about landscape architecture is that it is always in the present. It manifests itself as a constant change of states, physical states. The manifestations can be wind, weather … There are two main issues in my work: to stretch the awareness of the present as far as possible through the use of physical matter. And to intensify the sensory experience in the time and space it occurs in. The past and the future are separated by an interval of time whose duration and extent depends on the distance between the observed phenomenon and the observer.'[15]

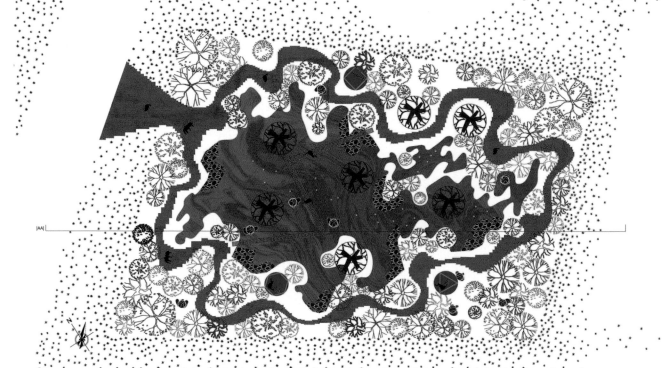

(Opposite) Stig Andersson, plan, Yellow Mud Garden, Xi'an International Horticultural Expo, China, 2010. Digital plan.
This rendering shows the continuing connection between landscape and painting.

Stig Andersson, collage perspective, Yellow Mud Garden, Xi'an International Horticultural Expo, China, 2010. Digital rendering.
A drawing using the convention of the vertical format common to Chinese art.

Lawrence Halprin (Lawrence Halprin and Associates)

Lawrence Halprin's notebook drawings trump all his office drawings. His observations of landscape, ideas jotted down in sketch form, and lively and colourful drawings used to persuade the public, are effective and clear. Some drawings include handwritten notes, some contain design ideas, and some have details of observed forms. His notebooks are the essence of his work. Halprin (1916–2009), born in New York City, established his office in San Francisco in 1949. More attuned to aesthetics and like other West Coast practitioners more exposed to Asian influences, he aligned himself aesthetically with the Modern Movement.

He stands out in two important ways. The first is the connection to movement that he had through his wife, the dancer and choreographer Anna Halprin. He invented a notation for her choreography and then extended that notation to the design of his fountains, to movement in his public spaces, and eventually even to choreographing public meetings for community-based design. 'The most important thing about designing is to generate creativity in others, and to be

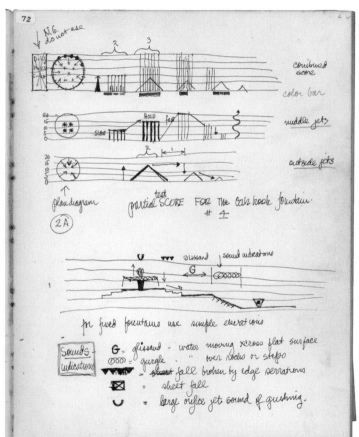

N.G. do not use

combined score

color bar

middle jets

HOLD fade

outside jets

plan diagram

2A

partial test SCORE FOR THE Oak brook fountain. #4

glissand   sound indications

G

for fixed fountains use simple elevations

Sounds indications

G = glissand - water moving across flat surface

= gurgle -   "   over rocks or steps

= sheet fall broken by edge serrations

= sheet fall

= large orifice jet sound of gushing.

Sea Ranch

MONDAY July 4th

Experiments in environment

workshop problem with church moore at Driftwood beach

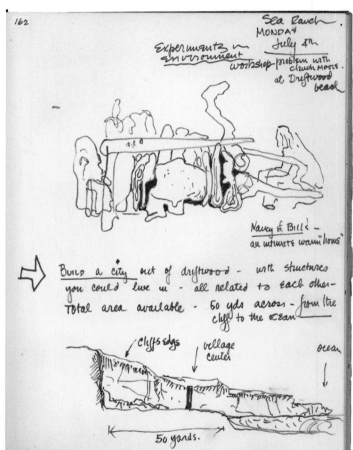

Nancy & Bill's - an intimate warm "home"

Build a city out of driftwood - with structures you could live in - all related to each other - Total area available - 50 yds across - from the cliff to the ocean

cliffs edge   village center   ocean

50 yards.

(Opposite left) Lawrence Halprin, partial test score for Oak Brook Fountain, undated. Pen on paper.
This drawing unites a choreographer's score with the representation of the landscape.

(Opposite right) Lawrence Halprin, Sea Ranch, experiments in environment workshop with Chuck Moore at Driftwood Beach, Marin County, California, USA, undated. Pen on paper.
This drawing is an early sketch that outlines the site constraints at Sea Ranch, a planned community on the California coast for which Halprin provided the master landscape plan. On the drawing Halprin notes the idea to 'Build a city out of driftwood – with structures you could live in – all related to each other ...'

Lawrence Halprin, sketch for Lovejoy Fountain Park, Portland, Oregon, USA, undated. Pen and watercolour on paper.
This sketch for Lovejoy Fountain Park bears the imperative that: 'In the plaza there should be events ... sculpture shows – concerts – dance events with dancers all over AND arriving to center space from above down stairs around [the] fountain ...'

inclusive – to include the needs and experiences of people interacting with the environment, and to let them be part of its creation,' Halprin wrote. 'And we finally get to a consensus, where you get a sense of what really ought to be done, and then they give it to me and then I draw it. I mean draw it in the philosophical sense. I sit down, work at it, because now I have a convincing feeling about what that place wants to be, you see? And it's not just me. Me and my talent comes in taking that consensus and then making something wonderful out of it – a work of art.'[16]

Halprin's spaces are choreographed, and their ties to dance are not superficial or merely decorative. He truly knew something about dance; not many landscape architects have a connection to that art. Anyone who has spent even a short time visiting Halprin's West Coast fountains and landscapes will recognise that he knew how to create spaces that put people in motion. For example, over a period of about four hours, his Ira Keller Fountain in Portland, Oregon, typically attracts acrobats, skaters, photographers,

energetic teenagers and well-dressed business people. As I observed, some climbed, some jumped, some splashed in the water and some sat sedately. But even those who only sat changed places frequently to see the water from different viewpoints.

The second way that Halprin stands apart from others is in his original use of notebooks. Although his office produced the measured drawings required for a project, and in some cases presented formal renderings, his notebook drawings steal the show. They were his main form of thinking and of developing, representing and communicating an idea. The exuberance of his lines and his vivid use of colour are unique among landscape designers. In his early office presentation drawings, he referenced Miró and other modern painters. In his mature work, the

(Opposite left) Lawrence Halprin, Lovejoy Fountain Park, Portland, Oregon, USA, 1966. Photograph.
Photographed in 2012, a park user shows the possibilities of movement and change inherent in the design of the fountain.

(Opposite right) Lawrence Halprin, possible wall for Portland fountain, c 1965–78. Pen and watercolour on paper.
Halprin's fascination with fractured ground would translate to poured-in-place concrete forms at Lovejoy Plaza and elsewhere. The sketch was made while Halprin was in the Sierra mountains.

Lawrence Halprin, waterfall in Partington Creek, Big Sur, California, USA, 1959. Pen on paper.
In this drawing, Halprin used different line weights to capture the movement of the water.

notebook drawings seem closer to Cubism. But Halprin is not derivative. One of his studies for the wall of the Ira Keller Fountain has the feel of Picasso's transformations of ordinary objects; Halprin takes the rock walls of the High Sierra and reinvents them.

Many landscape designers in the 1960s worked with coloured magic markers. But while that work today has a negative association, Halprin's use of magic marker for his notebook drawings makes it a credible artistic medium. His drawings seem to stand apart in their expressivity as well as in their informality, which may have been a reflection of life in California during those years. Placing Halprin's work in that context might appear to be derogatory, but it is the opposite; unlike the psychedelic art of that time, his work was knowledgeable and precise. He knew what he was after.

As most notebooks do, Halprin's contain travel drawings, but he elevated his by developing his observations into designs. It is also worth noting that he included sections as well as sketches of the historic sites he visited. Sections are fundamental drawings in landscape, though not much attention is paid to them. Among Halprin's drawings of the theatre at Delphi, for example, there is a little section that is dimensioned, showing the 3-foot (900-millimetre) distance between seats and the 1-foot (300-millimetre) difference in height between ground level and the seats.

In spite of Halprin's many urban commissions and the fame of his California Sea Ranch project and West Coast public spaces, the Eastern US establishment never quite viewed his work as central to landscape architecture. He was considered just a very good fountain designer. Though he won the important commission for the FDR Memorial in Washington, DC, it has never been regarded as one of his first-rate works.

Nonetheless, his fountains are indeed of particular interest. In his notebooks, Halprin dealt with fountains expressively, dedicating

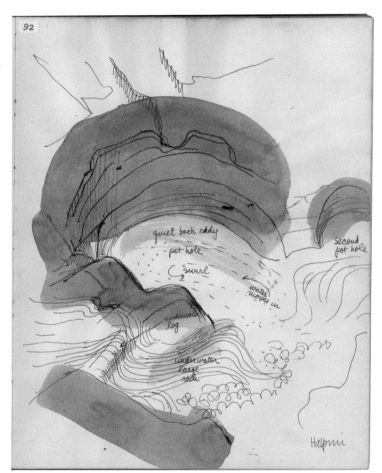

Lawrence Halprin, river, pothole and eddy, 1960. Pen and watercolour on paper. Halprin was influenced by what the Hungarian artist and Bauhaus teacher László Moholy-Nagy termed 'vision in motion'. Halprin developed 'motation' to document and diagram imagined movement through space and time in the landscape.

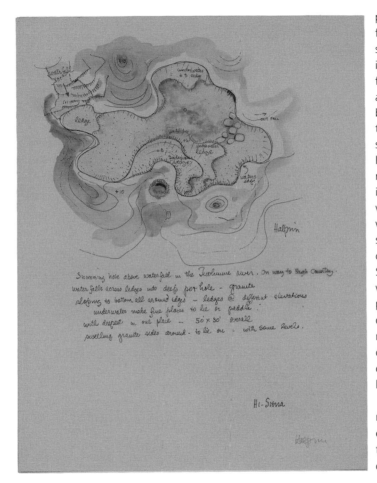

Lawrence Halprin, swimming hole above waterfall, 1960. Pen on paper.
Halprin's interest in water's movement in a drawing of a swimming hole on the High Sierras.

page after page to the study of water forms and movement. The notation system for movement that he invented is a completely new representation form for landscape design and deserves attention. But his fountains go a step beyond that. If you are familiar with the High Sierra, you can see a very sophisticated representation of that landscape in them. And it is not a romantic interpretation. After all, he is not even building with stone, but with ordinary concrete. That choice would hardly seem to be a recipe for success, given the highway-quality concrete generally used in the United States. And yet, he creates not just waterfalls with his fountains, but places that communicate the beauty of the landscape in which he spent many months of his life, travelling and observing. The fountains reach the level of high art in their representation of a landscape.

I have wondered about how much of an Asian influence there was on West Coast practitioners, and about the importance of the miniaturisation of landscapes – from bonsai to Chinese garden porcelain figures – to their work. But this is simply conjecture. Whether it reflects the Asian practice of the miniaturisation of a landscape or not, the reality of Halprin's Ira Keller Fountain is that it is an abstract non-referential representation of the High Sierra, a vernacular local landscape that feels familiar, and yet is not imitative in any way.

Diana Balmori (Balmori Associates)

Born in Spain, brought up in Spain and England, teenager and university student in architecture in Argentina, PhD in urban history from UCLA, landscape from Radcliffe. At the Yale School of Architecture, Critic in Landscape History (1992–5), Lecturer in Architecture (2000–2003), William B and Charlotte Shepherd Davenport Visiting Professor of Architectural Design (spring 2004), William Henry Bishop Visiting Professor of Architectural Design (autumn 2008/autumn 2010/autumn 2012). Lecturer at the Yale School of Forestry and Environmental Studies (1990–2007).

A better description of my education: a child's bilingual life between England and Spain, a teenager and adult between Argentina and the USA, growing up with intense Greek and Latin training, travelling to American Indian sites in South America with linguist father, on music and lecture tours and singing with my musician mother. My mother's brother was an English architect and city planner and she encouraged me in that direction. Nobody had heard of landscape architecture in the University of Tucumán where I studied, but it was the best architecture school in Argentina, destroyed soon after by military intervention. An extremely good Argentine painter, Ideal Sánchez, taught us drawing and painting. He took us to the mountains early in the morning where we had to draw and paint all day and at the end of the day we had a pin-up. The architecture professors were good too, but they did not like women in their studios and the one other woman and I were always left to the very end of the crit, and were frequently skipped altogether. It was the drawing and painting courses that stayed with me. Ideal Sánchez was a painter with a Surrealist and Metaphysical first period, then went on to Figurative painting. He never imposed on us style or method, only discussed ideas and concepts about form. From him I retained a clear sense of the intent of a drawing.

In representation my intention is to design space, not objects within a space, and to move landscape forward from background to foreground. This eliminates all delineating edges and gives priority to space. A Paul Cézanne quote in an exhibition of his late work – 'I concentrate, as I have gotten older, on the sensations of color and not the edges of the objects' – froze me in my steps on reading it, since I was seeking the same in our renderings.[17] Colour sensation was critical to the space imagined, establishing character and feeling.

The spaces depicted are programmed over time in different ways, this is conveyed in words or in thumbnail sketches. We leave this unspecified in the rendering, to avoid filling it with images of standard and fixed time-worn illustrations of the latest recreation fad in public space, always being about recreation.

As to our working concept about nature, we are inclusive. Not only do we include all living things and elements of the natural world, but also what we as humans create *if* it is made to function as nature. Imitating the *behaviour* of nature, rather than following the Picturesque tradition of emulating its appearance, provides a path towards comprehending living systems and representing them. This understanding is beginning to filter into design through biocomputation, the introduction of the behaviour of living systems through computing.

Our process of representation goes through the usual phases. First, there is drawing for oneself. Then there is drawing to capture an idea; these early sketches are part of everyday work. They range from making crude pencil lines, to coloured pencil studies of the tiers of a multi-level project, to outlines on a Photoshopped image of an existing site, that make the sketch more readable but introduce realistic imagery when the work is still inchoate and imprecise. This stage serves first to try to make a thought visible, and second to communicate it within the office. These sketches are developed and when they evolve, the drawing and

representation are meant for people who are not involved in creating the design – that is, for an external audience. At this point, depictions generally have to become more explicit, although representation is always symbolic. It is the idea behind the drawing, not the drawing itself, that is real. If you think of a drawing

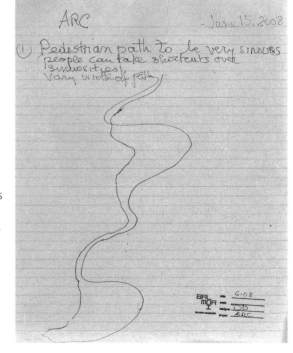

Diana Balmori, sketch for American Revolution Center, Valley Forge, Pennsylvania, USA, 2008. Pen on lined paper.
Early sketch.

as something you will see built, literally, you will be disappointed. But this is the claim of superrealistic renderings, and their claim to legitimacy.

The last stage of representation – the representation of our design intention for people outside the office – is entirely digital. The process of representation is about developing an idea, first defining the intention and exploring its constraints, and then inventing a form for it. A sophisticated patron can accept, even welcome, an abstract expression of

116

(Opposite left) Balmori
Associates, sketch for
Shenzhen Cultural Park,
China, 2003. Colour pencil
on paper.
Study for a multi-level park in
Shenzhen, China.

(Opposite right) Diana
Balmori, sketch for the High
Line Park Competition, New
York City, New York, USA,
2004. Digital rendering and
coloured pencil.
Sketch drawn over a computer-
generated image.

Balmori Associates, Wild &
Us Competition, St Patrick's
Island, Calgary, Canada,
2012. Digital rendering.
A drawing to depict space itself,
rather than the objects in it.

the ineffable. But the public,
still embracing a 19th-century
Picturesque aesthetic, wants to
see ahead of time exactly what
the landscape architect is going
to do and in general demands a
realistic rendering.

Overall we have four
aims in our search for ways to
represent our projects:

Space: we seek ways
of representing landscape as
space. We choose different
strategies to impart the feeling
of the flow of it and to undo
the objects in it, blurring or
erasing their edges. Among
other methods, we have used
a dot matrix, which allows the
space to flow around each dot,
and we have juxtaposed strong
patterns of similar value against
each other. Treating the whole
surface with a dot matrix, or
with whatever we use as a basic
algorithm to depict everything
in the drawing, is also a way
to move the background to
the foreground, changing

Balmori Associates, square,
Accrington, Lancashire,
England, 2007. Digital
rendering.
This rendering for a competition
entry uses a dot matrix
representational strategy to blur
the sharp contours of objects.

(Opposite) Balmori
Associates, Wild & Us
Competition, St Patrick's
Island, Calgary, Canada,
2012. Digital rendering.
This perspectival rendering
breaks the traditional
conventions of foreground,
middle ground and background
through the use of colour.

the traditional relation of landscape as background. However, we remain firmly attached to the horizon line – a fundamental part of any landscape – so that

the representation remains anchored in some form of realism and does not become totally abstract. It is a hybrid, referencing the real world but abstracting

Balmori Associates,
Wave Garden, 9th China
International Garden
Expo, Beijing, China,
2012. Conceptual digital
rendering.
Bands of planting like three-
dimensional brushstrokes.

Balmori Associates,
Wave Garden, 9th China
International Garden Expo,
Beijing, China, 2012. Digital
rendering.
Dissolving edges through the
variety of layers and patterns.

Balmori Associates,
residential complex, Tong
Shan, Shanghai, China, 2011.
Digital rendering.
Similar and dissimilar values
juxtaposed in order to represent
space.

Balmori Associates, Diana,
Princess of Wales Memorial
Fountain Competition,
London, England, 2001.
Photoshop rendering.
The linearity and serene quality
of the water plane contrast
with the dynamic stream.

its objects. This has given rise to many experiments in moving back and forth between abstraction and realism in representation. We have also used photographic realism at times to test the limits of making space predominate.

Colour: part of the world of sensation rather than that of thought, colour is difficult to explain in terms of its importance in representation. It is of great importance in our work, imparting character and creating a different way to approach a landscape. We spent an enormous amount of time in representing our work in the Botanical Research Institute of Texas to portray how intense colour becomes in the light of Texas, but giving too a sensation of changes in the light or in the planting colours. Handling colour is a physical sensation, it gives delight, and the difference in how colour is affected when light is very horizontal from when it is nearly vertical is dramatic. Colours communicate states of mind, and exposure to colour, intense colour, particularly in the warm colour range from yellow to red, feels as if it is emanating from the surface and advancing towards you as a physical presence, like wind does; you feel its presence though you do not see it. It comes as no surprise that in the American Indian cosmology the four directions east, west, north and south are considered to have a colour.

Interface: in seeking to emphasise space, we have also tried to break down the separation of buildings and landscape – object and space – to create the feeling that the two are, if not on a continuum, at least integrated. This is part of my work on interface with architect Joel Sanders. We have collaborated in studio work and commissions to merge architecture and landscape, to break with the usual division expressed by the contract line that establishes a 5-foot (1.5-metre) area outside a building where landscape designers can work, while the rest of a site is the architect's realm. We have co-authored a book, *Groundwork: Between Landscape and Architecture,* which looks at other contemporary examples of the blending of the two disciplines, marking the reassessment of their relationship.[18] In our joint attempts to find a way to integrate buildings and landscape, we have concentrated on the line between them, making the section at that line the most critical part of the representation of a project. The section allows you to reveal what is below the surface, how the contours are used, how they overlap with those uses, and how they intersect with architecture or infrastructure. Focusing on the section also forces you to bring the scale down to human dimensions and to move away from diagrams into design.

But the idea of interfacing and interlacing feeds all the forms and in fact the form is generated by this interlacing of a site with its context, by the interfacing with the architecture, by the interlacing with a river, a forest, or infrastructure.

Balmori Associates and
Joel Sanders, sections for
10 Li Park Competition,
Public Administrative Town,
South Korea, 2007. Digital
rendering.
10 Li Park evolved from the
overlay and intersection of a
central park and a linear park
on a perfect circle.

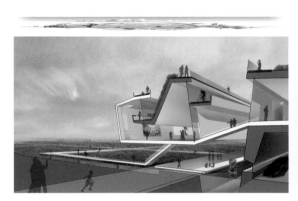

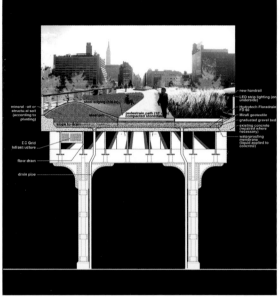

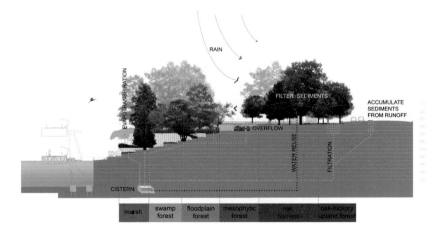

Balmori Associates, Beale
Street Landing Park,
Memphis, Tennessee, USA,
2008. Digital section.
This section shows the six
distinct Western Tennessee
plant communities, based on
levels of inundation by the
Mississippi River, and the water
recycling system.

Balmori Associates, High
Line Park Competition, New
York City, New York, USA,
2004. Digital rendering and
perspectival section.
The section provides technical
information while the
perspective provides a sense
of space.

(Opposite) Balmori
Associates, Botanical
Research Institute of Texas,
Fort Worth, Texas, USA,
2008.
Colour studies, a series.

Balmori Associates, process
for the rendering of
residential complex, Tong
Shan, Shanghai, China, 2012.
Process of the build-up of a
Rhino model and Photoshop
rendering.

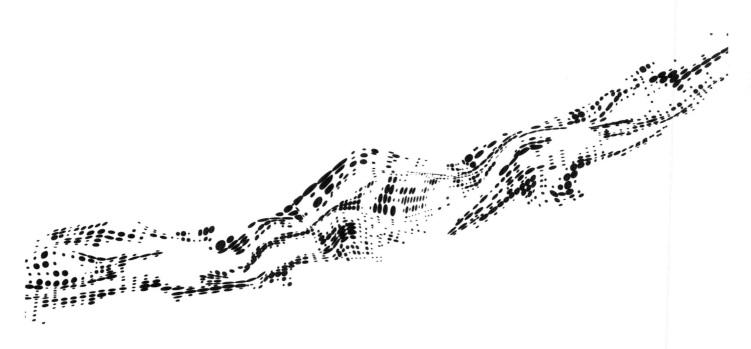

Visual data representation: we have set out to find a way to take the data on which a design is based and represent it visually, integrating it into the rendering. This is a new artistic form of diagramming for us. In our work, computer-generated diagrams play the role of representing complex ideas clearly and simply. They are sometimes used to depict a variety of programmes at a site, layered information – usually the development of a process over time, or the integration of plan and elevation. Our design for a garden in Beijing built in 2013 illustrates this method of representing data. In trying to express how the topography creates greatly different levels of exposure to sunlight in various parts of the garden, we used different colours in the computer drawing; the darkest blues and greens showed the areas that received the

Balmori Associates, The Bund Competition, Shanghai, China, 2007. Digital diagram. A sculpted topography mediates between the river and views across the city.

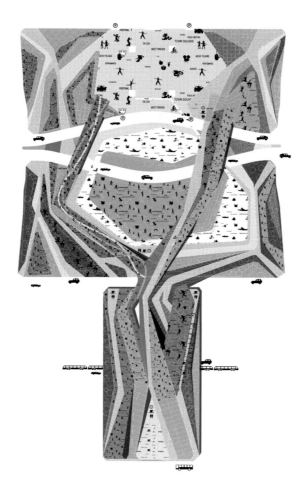

Balmori Associates, Shenzhen Cultural Park, China, 2003. Digital diagram. This diagram emphasises how the park, a fluid connector of green systems, can be used for multiple activities and as a conveyor of pedestrians, bikers and skaters, among others.

least sun, while the reds and yellows indicated the areas that received the most light. In another drawing for the same garden, the change in the size of the plantings was portrayed as they grew from shrubs to small trees to large trees over a four-year period. In still another, the different spot elevations of the site were expressed numerically, with the numbers making up the drawing itself. In other words, the drawing in all these cases represents the data that shape the design. We had been looking for a way to do that, and in 2011 Moa Carlsson, a graduate student at MIT who was a summer intern in our office and who shared our interest in computer representation as an artistic tool, taught us how.

Two earlier models also influenced our search for a way to represent a landscape through symbols of the underlying data. The first was Alexander von Humboldt's (1769–1859) illustrations that showed data about the relation of plants and animals to altitude on a mountain.

In the late 18th century, various innovative forms of representation were introduced, instigated by Denis Diderot's (1713–1784) *Encyclopédie*, which had as its original intention to tie image and text, but the technology and cost of printing kept the two apart.[19] Of the many efforts spurred by Diderot, those of Humboldt were the most important and successful. They

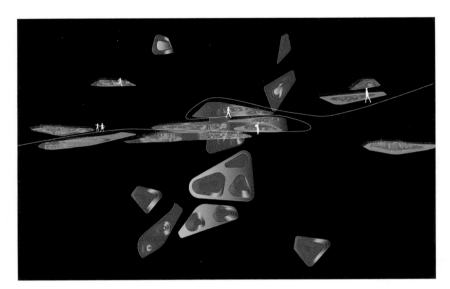

Balmori Associates, VIOL
Headquarters, São Paulo,
Brazil, 2012. Digital
rendering and plan.
Integration of plan and
elevation in one image.

Balmori Associates, study
of Detroit, Michigan, USA,
2010. Digital diagram.
This diagram of Detroit both
stacks and pulls apart studies
of infrastructure, soil type,
vegetation and vacancy
into layers, making the
proposal for interventions
understandable. This method
evokes Ian McHarg's mid-
20th-century mapping and
diagramming techniques.

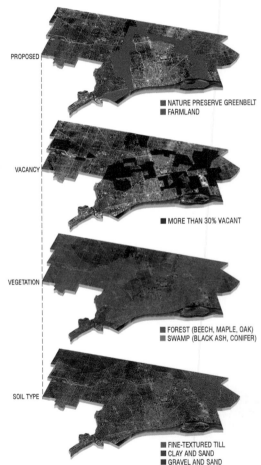

PROPOSED

■ NATURE PRESERVE GREENBELT
■ FARMLAND

VACANCY

■ MORE THAN 30% VACANT

VEGETATION

■ FOREST (BEECH, MAPLE, OAK)
■ SWAMP (BLACK ASH, CONIFER)

SOIL TYPE

■ FINE-TEXTURED TILL
■ CLAY AND SAND
■ GRAVEL AND SAND

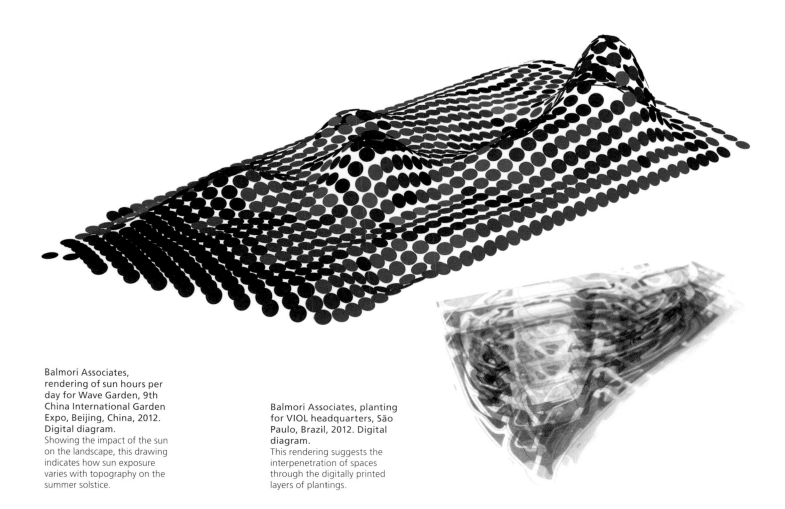

Balmori Associates,
rendering of sun hours per
day for Wave Garden, 9th
China International Garden
Expo, Beijing, China, 2012.
Digital diagram.
Showing the impact of the sun
on the landscape, this drawing
indicates how sun exposure
varies with topography on the
summer solstice.

Balmori Associates, planting
for VIOL headquarters, São
Paulo, Brazil, 2012. Digital
diagram.
This rendering suggests the
interpenetration of spaces
through the digitally printed
layers of plantings.

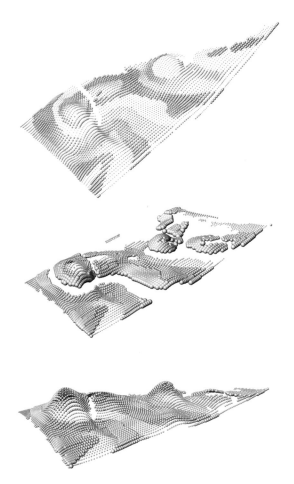

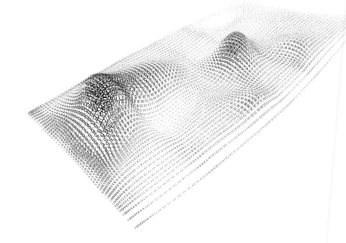

Balmori Associates, rendering of the site planted with bands of different species, years 1, 3 and 4 for Wave Garden, 9th China International Garden Expo, Beijing, China, 2012. Digital diagram.
This image shows how various trees will grow over a four-year period. Diagramming the information enables an understanding of the volumetric impact of growth.

Balmori Associates, rendering of the slope condition of the site for Wave Garden, 9th China International Garden Expo, Beijing, China, 2012.
The parametric of numbers in this rendering indicates the spot elevations of the site and creates an image of the landscape.

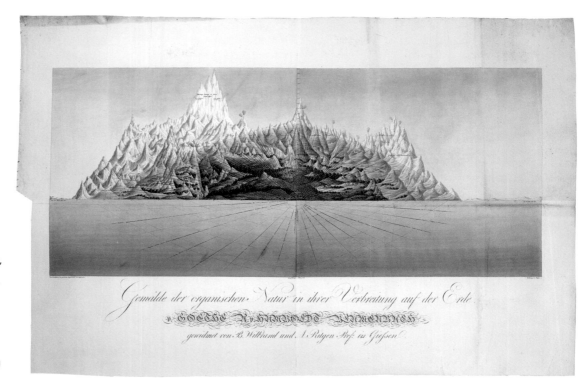

Joseph Paringer (based on original work by Ferdinand August von Ritgen and Johann Bernhard Wilbrand), worldwide distribution of organic nature, 1821. Hand-coloured lithograph.
The long search for visual representation of a landscape and its data extends back to the 19th century. Paringer in this drawing was interested in representing data and creating an artistic image.

generated many similar efforts, such as the one by Ferdinand August von Ritgen (1787–1867) and Johann Bernhard Wilbrand (1749–1846) that is illustrated here. Why did Humboldt and his contemporaries spend so much effort on these illustrations when they could

have presented the data much more easily in a chart? In his famous *Essay on the Geography of Plants with a Physical Tableau of the Equinoctial Region*, Humboldt stated, 'I thought that if my Tableau were capable of suggesting unexpected analogies it would also be

speaking to the imagination and providing the pleasure that comes from contemplating nature.' As Sylvie Romanowski notes, in keeping with Humboldt's vision of an analytical as well as holistic visually oriented science, his overriding concern was the tight integration of text and image.[20] Beyond that, he also wanted to create an innovative and aesthetically pleasing way of presenting data. In addition, he wanted the viewer to be an active participant in the illustration, correlating the data with the picture. His tableau became a model of successful representation of science data in text and images, which emerged from a discipline akin to what today we would consider ecology.

Charles Joseph Minard (1781–1870), the French engineer, also worked during this time. His well-known illustration, drawn in 1869, shows the terrible fate of Napoleon's army in Russia. It combines a data map and time-series, showing in a tan flow-line the size of the Grand Army of 422,000 men. The width of the band diminishes to 100,000 when it reaches Moscow, and by the time the army struggled back to Poland it is represented by a thin line indicating that only 10,000 men were left. Edward Tufte has said that it may well be the best statistical graphic ever drawn.[21]

The second model was the work of Chinese painter Xu Bing, who has created landscape images

Xu Bing, Landscript, 2001. Painting, album leaf, ink on paper.
A landscape composed of Chinese characters emerges in Xu Bing's painting.

using Chinese calligraphy. Looking at his work, I saw a parallel to our own search for a method of using a symbolic language to create a representation of a landscape. A famous poster by Ryuichi Yamashiro in the MoMA collection, *Forest* (1954), created at the height of the concrete poetry movement, drew a forest using the glyphs for 'tree'. This approach to representation has been the focus of our most recent representation effort.

Unlike most projects in our office, the masterplan for the Public Administration City in Sejong, Korea (MPPAT) was designed mostly digitally, partly because of our agreement to work together with Haeahn Architecture and H Associates (who were in charge of architecture) to try to make the landscape and architecture of Sejong Administration City seamless, and also because the project was for an international competition, not a commission. The competition was to design a new city on the Han River about two hours south of Seoul and relocate about half of the national government ministries there. The idea behind it was to relieve overcrowding in Seoul and drive growth in the rest of the country. We won the competition in 2007. Working on tracing

paper in pencil on top of a plan of the site, we came up with the main idea for the project during our first planning session: the ministries would all be under one roof in a linear configuration, using the river to generate its form. The next step, which began to give the project form, was generated parametrically in a process called tangential evolution, taking lines

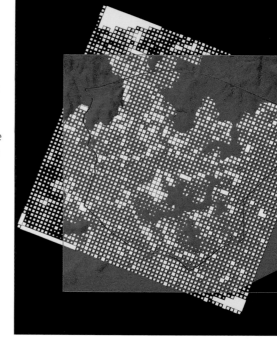

Balmori Associates, masterplan for Public Administration City, Sejong, South Korea, 2006. Digital rendering.
The existing topography informs the organisation of open spaces and green infrastructure.

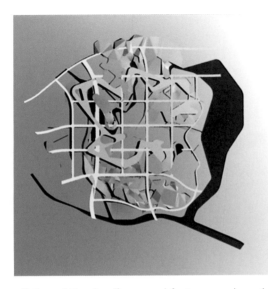

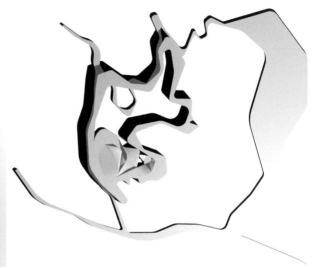

Balmori Associates, masterplan for Public Administration City, Sejong, South Korea, 2006. Digital rendering.
This drawing was made to understand how the form of the site – its parameters – could be used to generate the form of the interventions.

Balmori Associates, masterplan for Public Administration City, Sejong, South Korea, 2006. Digital rendering.
The second phase of our design for Sejong involved removing lines from the existing landforms and features.

off the existing landforms and features, such as the river and roads, and rationalising them as tangents. Our intention was to make the natural elements on the site evolve into built form. The plan was also flexible and could be developed in phases, growing in a way somewhat similar to chaos theory, with the tangents spinning off endlessly. In the MPPAT project, as a tangent met a feature, it was redirected and transformed so that it grew organically out of its parameters; the result is the shape we see. The topography came first. The site's extant infrastructure, such as the grid of roads, came second, and the playful interaction between the river and the extended continuous roof covering all 11 ministries, third.

Our masterplan was only for the governmental city of Sejong; we had no control over its surroundings. All the residential buildings around the administrative city would be in the form of towers grouped together as a village, seen in the background of the perspective. We decided a major aim was to offer contrast by having the buildings of the administrative city no higher than six storeys, conveying the image of an accessible government. As a second aim we sought the continuous roof to

(Opposite) Balmori Associates, masterplan for Public Administration City, Sejong, South Korea, 2006. Digital plan.

make a case for having the different ministries connect to each other and thereby communicate with one another. We also sought to interlace ground with roof park, a place from which to see the surrounding mountains and rice fields. But while topographic and landscape aims could be partially shown, a social agenda could not be represented; there is no digital format for such cross-disciplinary information. The image of the buildings depicted in orange in the plan only represents the continuous rooftop park.It is a project that interlaces with what surrounds it – the apartment towers and the rice fields (part of the water cleaning system) – and that interweaves and juxtaposes the transit grid that already existed with the narrow pedestrian roads – not configured as a grid – that we laid over it.

Sejong is a new kind of city because of its masterplan. In contrast, the 1956 masterplan of Brasília resulted in a monumental, inhospitable administrative city, though with extremely good buildings designed by Oscar Niemeyer. When it is finished in 2015, Sejong will offer a very livable and

Balmori Associates, masterplan for Public Administration City, Sejong, South Korea, 2006. Digital rendering.
A continuous roof over all ministries (in orange).

(Opposite) Balmori Associates, Bilbao Abandoibarra, Bilbao, Spain, 2012. Digital rendering.
City, mountain, river and site (orange).

new city, though its buildings will lack the quality of Brasília's.

Our masterplan for Abandoibarra in Bilbao, Spain, involved joining the area of Bilbao's port to the city's very centre and opening up the city to the river. A small industrial city, Bilbao, the Detroit of Spain (though with shipbuilding rather than automotive industry as its economic base), had the good fortune of having innovative mayors who used every opportunity to improve the city. When the port was moved from the centre of the city to the mouth of the Nervión river, the mayor led an effort to set up a public-private organisation, Bilbao Ria 2000, and leveraged international, national and Basque monies and interests to reorganise Bilbao as a city from scratch.

The reshaping of Bilbao began with an international competition that we won (along with two architectural firms, Pelli Clarke Pelli Architects and Aguinaga & Associates). We were responsible for all the outdoor spaces and transport, the latter in conjunction with very able and enlightened local transport engineers. The first thing to go up was Gehry's Guggenheim Museum, which communicated the image of a new Bilbao.

The site we worked on can be seen in orange in this representation of the whole city with its mountains. It is a poetic image that powerfully conveys our sense of Bilbao – a town nestled between mountains along a river, with a longing for the sea. The city is spatially dense and lacks open space. The opening to the river seemed to provide an infusion of Bilbao's seafaring history and a relief from the city's density. In every representation of each of the spaces we designed – Plaza Euskadi (the central plaza) and Campa de los Ingleses Park (Campa), respectively a commission and an international competition first prize – we sought this infusion of the river, sea air and open space throughout. A series of representations of these new spaces sought to communicate the spaciousness we were seeking for Bilbao. In our winning entry for Campa, we accomplished this by making multiple paths wind their way to the river and to the linear park along its edge, using park ribbons, as seen in this plan and in a

Balmori Associates, Campa de los Ingleses Park, Bilbao, Spain, 2007. Digital rendering.
This bird's-eye perspectival rendering conveys how the park comes down in ribbons to the river.

computer sketch interpreting the main ramp as a floral garland. We designed Plaza Euskadi so that it moves towards the river like a river itself, with calm slower pools flowing out of the main busy current along its sides; this photograph shows the just-finished space in early 2012. When mayor Iñaki Azkuna inaugurated Plaza Euskadi, the ceremony started with a Basque regional dance performed by a dancer all in white with a red band around his waist; it seemed to be a fitting event for the space.

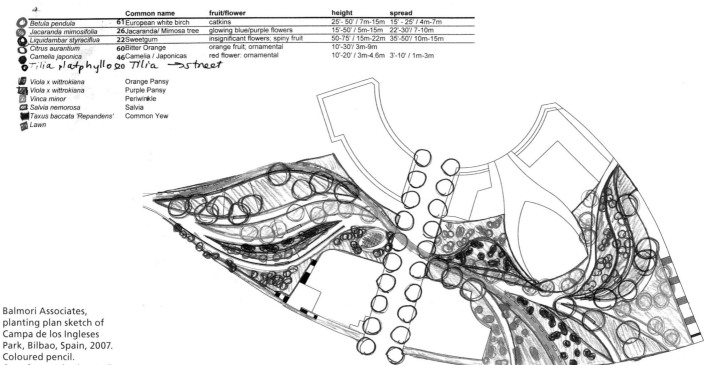

	Common name	fruit/flower	height	spread
Betula pendula	61 European white birch	catkins	25'- 50' / 7m-15m	15' - 25' / 4m-7m
Jacaranda mimosifolia	26 Jacaranda/ Mimosa tree	glowing blue/purple flowers	15'-50' / 5m-15m	22'-30' / 7-10m
Liquidambar styraciflua	22 Sweetgum	insignificant flowers; spiny fruit	50-75' / 15m-22m	35'-50' / 10m-15m
Citrus aurantium	60 Bitter Orange	orange fruit; ornamental	10'-30'/ 3m-9m	
Camelia japonica	46 Camelia / Japonicas	red flower: ornamental	10'-20' / 3m-4.6m	3'-10' / 1m-3m

Tilia platphyllo 20 Tilia →street

Viola x wittrokiana	Orange Pansy
Viola x wittrokiana	Purple Pansy
Vinca minor	Periwinkle
Salvia nemorosa	Salvia
Taxus baccata 'Repandens'	Common Yew
Lawn	

Balmori Associates, planting plan sketch of Campa de los Ingleses Park, Bilbao, Spain, 2007. Coloured pencil.
One of many planting studies.

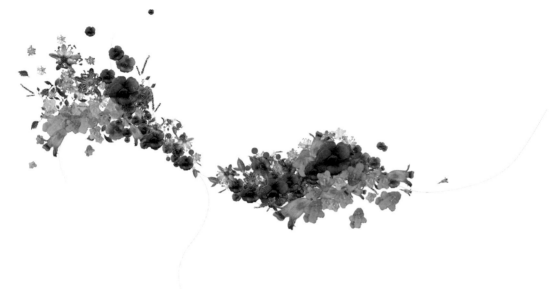

Balmori Associates, Campa de los Ingleses Park, Bilbao, Spain, 2007. Digital collage, colour patterned papers.

The aim of the entire design was to interlace the river and the old city with the new piece of urban land from the old port. But how was it to be expressed? Images we created for Euskadi included one of the main plaza which aligns the central path with the road to the river. Our design does not aim to be like the old city. Its aim is to weave in park and river and venues for people to move through it, feeling that their city is beautiful. All the paths and resting spots point towards the river. What beauty may consist of in this case may be having them see the river as for the first time.

Summary

A brief look at the design aims, forms of representation and interpretations of nature of each of these practitioners shows great differences among them in all four categories. These range from Landscape Urbanists understanding nature as process and using diagrams

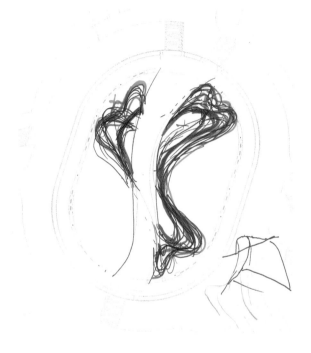

Diana Balmori, sketch of
Plaza Euskadi, Bilbao, Spain,
2009. Marker on paper.
Three public park side 'pockets'
are attached to the central
path.

Balmori Associates, Plaza
Euskadi, Bilbao, Spain, 2009.
Digital plan.
A direct central path is the
focus of the energy and urban
movement towards the river.

as a way of representing it, to Bernard Lassus seeing landscape as a process in a viewer's mind and rejecting its representation altogether.

In nearly all of these practices, the perception of time appears as an important dimension. For the Landscape Urbanists, the focus becomes *development* over time, which implies continuity. For all the others,

however, the focus is on *change* over time, which implies discontinuity. In most of these practices, there is also a new attention paid to how the landscape is perceived or sensed and a questioning of whether there is an ultimate reality independent of human perception. Accordingly, there is an emphasis on the mental or sensory paths through which the landscape is apprehended. In Lassus's work, this takes the form of theoretical ideas about perception and of the primacy of direct experience. In Andersson's practice, it is seen in the attention to the direct effect of the landscape on the senses – tactile, aural, olfactory and visual. In my office's work, it is evident in the focus on the critical role of peripheral vision in allowing you to appreciate and understand landscape.

For all these practitioners, a definitive change in attitude towards nature has taken place, though each of them expresses it differently. Johanson's understanding of nature transforms the role of art so that it supports all the forms of life present on the site; in her work, aesthetics serves ecology and fosters the public's understanding of it. In Haag's practice, his view of nature takes the form of an acceptance of everything on the site, eliminating the separation between artificial and natural. In Andersson's work, it is expressed by registering all the qualities of nature present in cities and drawing attention to them through creating different sensory experiences. In my practice, it is reflected in seeing nature as a living system which can be emulated and put to work by means of engineered solutions.

It is the aims of these practitioners that vary most dramatically and give the clearest sense of the

vast changes that the discipline is undergoing. Their practices do have a common denominator; most of the work ignores the great outdoors and the suburbs and is instead concentrated in the densest areas of large cities. In addition, there is an ecological basis for all their aims. Other than that, however, there are enormous differences in both the specific aims and the means to accomplish them. For Landscape Urbanists, the aim is the re-creation of the city itself,

Balmori Associates, Bilbao Abandoibarra, Bilbao, Spain, 2012. Photo by Iwan Baan of Plaza Euskadi at its completion.

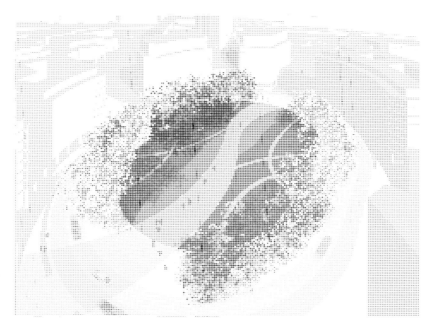

Balmori Associates, Plaza Euskadi, Bilbao, Spain, 2006. Digital rendering.
The Plaza emerges as a pivot that unifies various built elements.

Andersson seeks to engage all the senses in experiencing public space in the city and considers them critical to people's enjoyment of it. His forms of representation have the same aim as his work: to convey all the sensory aspects of the site. Johanson aims to have her landscapes function ecologically, using aesthetics to reveal a complex living world that is not easily seen through traditional designs. Her notebook drawings depict a seemingly figurative, fantastic landscape, although because of their scale, the figures cannot be perceived literally. She creates an *Alice in Wonderland* landscape in which the scales of the figures make a forest out of a meadow. She is the hermeneutist, translating her discoveries through the language of art.

Bernard Lassus's aim is the most abstract, for he sees landscape as the direct experience of a site, shaped by the idea of how it is perceived. His art lies in the way he configures the space to allow the public

at the level of urban design and planning, achieved through mapping and diagramming. Since Haag's aim is to reveal a site, he intervenes directly there and avoids creating representations of it. He sees final renderings as visual swindles.[22] Halprin seeks a communal vision of urban public space that engages users kinesthetically and strives to involve them in the design. His representation has a notebook character and communicates his ideas informally.

to see his perception of the real site. He is against any form of representation of this perception, which he believes is only revealed by the work on the site itself. For my office's practice, conveying the spatial quality of a space trumps all other aims. And because space is an emptiness and in certain ways evanescent – an aura rather than a thing – it is very difficult to convey. Representation therefore is both much more critical to our work and more difficult to understand.

It is possible to name the many qualities of the space to be designed, but they are not fixed; rather, the space is shaped for users to interpret and to explore, discovering the ways it can be enjoyed. The space seeks to interlace with all those things around it which can augment life in it and to disengage from what detracts from life there. It may be superfluous to state that this work deals with urban space, whose creation nearly always requires pushing other things aside. It is about opening up a space for the public – for the demos – and democracy. I recall these words, from 17th-century Germany, which I heard in a graduate school seminar led by historian HH Liang: 'City air makes you free.' That is what we seek for our spaces: to have them be like opening a door in a city and letting water and air and people run freely through it.

Balmori Associates, Parque de La Luz, Las Palmas, Gran Canaria, Spain, 2005. Photocollage.
Proposed connectivity between the port, the park and the city.

References

1 George Santayana, *The Sense of Beauty*, Charles Scribner's Sons (New York), 1896.

2 John Dixon Hunt, '"Ut Pictura Poesis": The Garden and the Picturesque in England (1710–1750)', in Monique Mosser and Georges Teyssot (eds), *The Architecture of Western Gardens: A Design History from the Renaissance to the Present Day*, MIT Press (Cambridge, MA), 1991, pp 231–42.

3 Ian Hamilton Finlay, *Cascade*, Wild Hawthorn Press (Edinburgh), 1993.

4 In a letter that Raphael wrote to Pope Leo X concerning his designs for St Peter's. Roger Jones and Nicholas Penny, *Raphael*, Yale University Press (New Haven, CT), 1983, p 216.

5 Charles Waldheim, 'A Reference Manifesto', in Charles Waldheim (ed) *The Landscape Urbanism Reader*, Princeton Architectural Press (New York), 2006, pp 13–19, see p 19.

6 James Corner, 'Terra Fluxus', in Charles Waldheim (ed), *The Landscape Urbanism Reader*, Princeton Architectural Press (New York), 2006, pp 21–33.

7 James Corner, 'Representation and Landscape, 1992', in *Theory in Landscape Architecture: A Reader*, Simon Swaffield (ed), University of Pennsylvania Press, 2002, pp 145–46.

8 Julia Czerniak, 'Challenging the Pictorial: Recent Landscape Practice', in *Assemblage*, no 34, MIT Press (Cambridge, MA), December 1997, pp 110–20.

9 Andrea Koenecke, Udo Weilacher and Joachim Wolschke-Bulmahn (eds), *Die Kunst, Landschaft Neu Zu Erfinden: Werk Und Wirken Von Bernard Lassus*, Martin Meidenbauer (Pieterlen, Switzerland), 2010.

10 Ian L McHarg, *Design with Nature*, John Wiley & Sons, Inc (New York), 1992.

11 From communication with the artist, 24 October 2012.

12 Ibid.

13 Xin Wu, *Patricia Johanson and the Re-Invention of Public Environmental Art, 1958–2010*, Ashgate (Surrey), 2013.

14 The comparison was drawn in an email communication from Michel Conan, 4 June 2013.

15 *SLA*, C3 Publishing Co (Seoul), 2007, pp 9, 11, 14.

16 Leslie McGuire, *In His Own Words: Lawrence Halprin*, LandscapeOnline, <http//www.landscapeonline.com/research/article/12990>.

17 The quote was transcribed at the exhibition *Cézanne in Provence* at the National Gallery of Art in Washington, DC, spring 2006.

18 Diana Balmori and Joel Sanders, *Groundwork: Between Landscape and Architecture*, Monacelli Press (New York), 2011.

19 Denis Diderot, *Encyclopédie, ou Dictionnaire Raisonné des Sciences, des Arts et des Métiers* (Paris), from 1751 to 1765.

20 Alexander von Humboldt and Aimé Bonpland, *Essay on the Geography of Plants*, edited with an introduction by Stephen T Jackson, trs by Sylvie Romanowski, University of Chicago Press (Chicago), 2009, pp 79, 188.

21 Edward R Tufte, *The Visual Display of Quantitative Information*, Graphics Press (Cheshire, CT), 2001, p 40.

22 Daniel Jost, 'Rich Haag Owes his Life to a Tree', *Landscape Architecture Magazine*, 28 March 2013.

5

Historical Issues in Landscape Architecture Representation

So what are the issues that we, as professionals, have to deal with concerning the representation of landscape? In my own view and in my own practice, I think there are five. The first is the continuing importance of painting. The second has to do with the representation of representation. The close connection that landscape has had with theatrical representation has left landscape with a complex language of representation of representation that is worth re-examining in relation to the depiction of space. The use of trompe l'oeil – a technique that was important in the past but that merits revisiting today – is another example of the representation of a representation related to landscape, as well as of the connection between landscape and painting. The third concerns the depiction of space itself, and in particular, the need to find formats that can encompass the large expanses with which

landscape now engages. The fourth is the use of integrated drawings. Finally, the fifth is the temporality of the ever-changing landscape – a dimension that neither drawing nor painting can capture, except imperfectly in sequential panels.

Given the new situation of landscape architecture, however, is the historical material relevant? In the 18th and 19th centuries, history was considered the discipline that best explained reality; people believed that you needed to know the history of something to understand it. Today, however, the prevalence of the conviction that reality is best described in scientific terms has led to the privileging of current knowledge and the devaluation of what preceded it. As a result, we no longer believe that comprehending history enables us to understand our own time. Nonetheless, understanding the history of landscape architecture's engagement with these five issues can help us to deal with them today.

Drawing and Painting

Though landscape painting and landscape design came into their own and began to function together as one art in the 17th century, there are some earlier examples of connections between them. Because the concept of nature was different in each period, it is not possible to compare the various roles of landscape representation. What is possible, however, is to see how important painting was to the representation of landscape across time and cultures.

With precedents in large-scale Hellenistic wall paintings, mural frescoes became important to the Romans during the 2nd century AD. Trompe-l'oeil representations of the landscape appeared in the so-called Second Style of Roman fresco painting by c 50–40 BC in the villa of Fannius Synistor at Boscoreale for example, when the Romans began to build country villas with inner courtyards open on one side to the surrounding landscape. Perhaps there is nothing as moving or beautiful as the fresco in Livia's villa (1st century BC) – now in the collection of the Palazzo Massimo alle Terme – of life-size young orange trees with a bird on one of the branches; it is overwhelming in its freshness and vigour. It is at one-to-one scale so you feel you are in front of a garden, not of a painting. Its vivid colours are part of its appeal, inviting you in.

Landscape also appears in the form of frescoes in the villas of the Renaissance. These frescoes often show not just the landscape of the owner's villa but surrounding villas and their landscapes as well. Unlike the eye-level views of the Roman frescoes, these are bird's-eye views, intended to show an entire estate with its landscape, working lands and buildings. The Renaissance fresco paintings sometimes continued indoors on the walls of the large public rooms. In addition, in some villas, the window shutters were painted on the inside with a view of the landscape outside the window; this trompe-l'oeil device was also important to landscape representation in later periods. Still another form of landscape painting in Renaissance villas is that of the Italian painter of Flemish origins Giusto Utens (1558–1609); his famous lunettes became the best-known representations of the landscapes of the most important Medici villas in Tuscany. Indeed, because of these lunettes, Utens became better known than the designers of the landscapes he painted.

The painted landscape representations in a villa were a form of display of their owner's power, but they were also considered an important aesthetic endeavour in their own right. The artists who painted the frescoes had nothing to do with those who designed the landscapes. Creating landscapes and representing them were separate undertakings with separate aims, although both were governed by aesthetic considerations. For example, Paolo Veronese's

frescoes that adorn the villa built by Andrea Palladio for Daniele Barbaro at Maser (1560–61) depict imaginary landscapes that reference ancient myths, rather than the actual landscape of the villa's working agricultural fields.

Landscape painting established itself as a genre in the 17th century, notably with the work of Claude Lorrain (1600–1682), but also with that of Nicolas Poussin (1594–1665) and Salvator Rosa (1615–1673). Their paintings presented images of 'countryside' rather than designed landscapes and had an overwhelming impact, particularly on the developing English landscape. Landscape design emerged as a separate discipline during this period as well. The garden had become an entity in itself during the Renaissance, but its designers were generally little known. Instead, *fontainiers*, horticulturalists, sculptors and others who designed the various elements that made gardens were more visible. And more often than not, the

Paolo Veronese, Landscape and dog, Villa Barbaro, Maser, Italy, completed *c* 1559. Fresco.
Veronese's paintings at Villa Barbaro show fictive landscapes rather than the villa's actual setting, intertwining painting and landscape design.

Hubert Robert, *The Tomb of Jean-Jacques Rousseau at Ermenonville*, 1802. Oil on canvas.
Robert not only painted Rousseau's tomb at Ermenonville, but he was also its designer.

owner of the garden was named as its designer, or at least credited with the idea for it. But by Louis XIV's time (1638–1715), that had changed, and the great Le Nôtre headed a team of all those who created the individual components of a garden, such as fountains, plantings and ornaments. The garden designer had clearly come into prominence.

Landscape painting set the rules that were adopted for designing landscapes and was the dominant landscape art from the late 17th century on. It was then that landscape painting became the generator of actual, physical landscapes. Such was the power of painting at that moment that the seemingly impossible happened: the representation became the real landscape. The work of Hubert Robert (1733–1808), who translated his pictorial strategies into built form, is a clear example of this. Robert, who trained as a painter and became a well-known artist, later designed many important landscapes, including the Grotte des Bains d'Apollon at Versailles. He also painted these landscapes – such as the one of Marquis René-Louis de Girardin's garden park at Ermenonville. One of its features is Jean-Jacques Rousseau's tomb, which was probably designed by Robert for a setting on an artificial island there.

The professional training of the first important landscape designers also contributed to the strong connection between landscape painting and landscape design. Like Robert, William Kent also trained as a painter, and Le Nôtre studied painting under Simon Vouet. In addition, Le Nôtre studied mathematical perspective, used the eighth theorem of Euclid's *Optics* in his work, and was familiar with the newly discovered concept of mathematical infinity discussed in Principle 27 of Descartes's *Les Principes de la Philosophie* (1644). As Le Nôtre's training also indicates, landscape was

immersed in all of the critical disciplines of his time; it was a fortunate period for the field. William Chambers (1723–1796), Architect to George III, noted that English landscape designers were 'not only botanists but also painters and philosophers'.[1]

Alexander Pope (1688–1744), the most important 18th-century English poet and satirist, translator of *The Iliad* and *The Odyssey*, and designer of his own influential garden in Twickenham, was adviser on many other important gardens. 'All gardening,' he said, 'is landscape painting.'[2] Humphry Repton (1752–1818), the inventor of the accomplished form of landscape representation shown in his 'Red Books', called himself 'a landscape painter and practical gardener'. Describing the way he worked, Repton wrote: 'visited the site, walking the ground with the Owner taking note of what the client wanted, sketching present and proposed scenes'.[3] At home, he turned his pen-and-ink sketches into watercolours, a favoured medium of his time and place. (The late 18th century was the era of watercolour, and Repton was from Norwich – the centre of the watercolour movement in England.)

It may be argued that a painting of an actual landscape that an artist is beholding has no real connection to the completely invented representation of a designed landscape that has not yet been built. But all representation is an abstraction; a painting of a landscape is not simply a copy of it. There are numerous examples of painters offering totally different representations of the same subject. That is, in bringing out features or qualities that may not be apparent to someone else looking at the same scene, the painter is also inventing a landscape. Moreover, landscape designers for their part do not create landscapes from scratch. They work with conditions of earth, stone, water and other features, the behaviour and form of which are familiar to them, although the designers may later modify those elements significantly.

Painters struggled over decades to unite foreground and background, from putting the human figure in the foreground and jumping directly to the distant background landscape in stark Renaissance portraits, to creating an intermediate plane – such as a balcony or gallery – to showing several planes, with things diminishing in scale to ultimately reach the horizon and the sky. That same struggle can also be seen in the design of real landscape. Through those efforts, painting established the rules of foreground, middle ground and background and of the horizontal stripes that receded into the background, uniting front and back. These rules were now applied on the ground by landscape designers, and would have a most immediate and important effect on English landscapes.

The discovery of the rules of perspective, including the spatial concepts of philosophers and mathematicians, brought new unity to all the visual arts and had a substantial effect on both painting

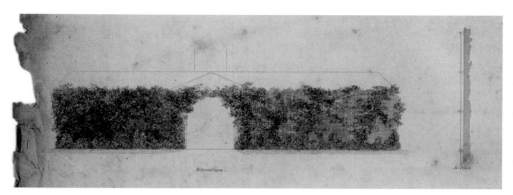

Elevation.

David Ramsay for John Claudius Loudon, A wall trellis, Kiddington House, Enstone, Oxfordshire, England, 1843. Pencil, pen and watercolour.
Painting in watercolour was a particularly strong tradition in the nineteenth century. In the last weeks of his life, Loudon designed a garden that included a rosarium. A draughtsman, David Ramsay, realised this depiction.

and garden design. In his *Traité du jardinage*, Jacques Boyceau explained that he considered the study of draughtsmanship, architecture and geometry essential to garden art.[4] And it was Donato Bramante's Cortile del Belvedere (begun in 1504–5 and completed in 1562–5) – a space in the Vatican Palace which is courtyard, garden and theatre – which became the most famous example of the organisation of a space based on a perspectival view.

By the beginning of the 19th century, painting had given rise to the most enduring landscape design aesthetic, the Picturesque. In *The Picturesque: Studies in a Point of View*, Christopher Hussey (1899–1970) recalls sitting in the library of his family home as a boy, looking out of the window at a composed English scene.[5] He reached for a book by Uvedale Price that his grandfather had read and discovered that his

grandfather had applied conventions that he had learned from pictures to the siting of the house, the planting of the garden and the view from the window. 'And before I read far,' writes Hussey, 'I reflected that all these scenes, which I instinctively called artistic, must be "picturesque".'[6] It is significant that he recognised that landscape design was taken from painting, but what is most surprising is that, as a result, he no longer considered the design to be artistic. His statement both clearly marks a change in the values that had prevailed until then, and is also an indication of what those values had been.

By 1800, a more complex landscape that created distinct spaces and invited the visitor to move through it was prioritised. Still embedded in the pictorial and theatrical tradition, these new spaces were conceived like a series of stage sets. But they set the visitor in motion and the kinesthetic experience rather than the visual one became important.

The Picturesque first made its mark on the English landscape, but then extended to Continental Europe and to America. Much vilified for its tenacious hold on the public's idea of what a landscape is, the Picturesque put an emphasis on the elements by which you move through a space, something that continues to be critical to this day.

Though by the mid-19th century landscape design began to separate itself from the arts, landscape plans were frequently painted in watercolours throughout the 19th century and early part of the 20th century; good examples of these are epitomised by the work of Gertrude Jekyll or John Claudius Loudon. And in the 20th century, the Brazilian landscape architect Roberto Burle Marx reintroduced modern painting into his renderings.

A knowledge of landscape representations that emerged from painting is therefore necessary to our understanding of the design of real landscapes. Another significant way in which painting has a prominent position in designed landscape is in the painted sets of landscapes for theatrical representation, as I will discuss fully later.

Representation of Representation: The Theatre in the Garden and the trompe l'oeil

Two historical forms of landscape representation, the theatre in the garden and the trompe l'oeil, illustrate the concept of the representation of landscape within a physical designed landscape. Before examining them, however, the first thing to mention is that all representation is a simulacrum. Drawing is a process by which one creates a simulation of something – a concept or a space, for example – in an effort to reveal its meaning or make it clear and intelligible. So a drawing is a simulacrum of whatever its subject is.

In the first example of representation of representation, representations of landscapes in theatre sets combine with the designed landscape around the theatre to form one ensemble with two layers of simulation. As their biographies show, the landscapers of the 17th century were connected to theatre as an art either through designing sets of painted landscapes for a play or through designing theatres in gardens. Landscapers' drawings for sets for these open-air

Gertrude Jekyll, The Copse in Brook, Godalming, Surrey, England, 1913. Watercolour on paper.
Jekyll was commissioned to create a garden in Surrey for RW Williamson in 1913. This watercolour shows the design of a marsh for the garden.

theatres have clear similarities to the drawings of sets by well-known theatre designers such as Inigo Jones (1573–1652) and Filippo Juvarra (1687–1736) (both also architects).

The simulacra reach a high point of refinement when theatre sets that mimic the landscape open up and combine with the existing garden, which in turn is transformed into a simulation, becoming part of the stage set. When real elements of a landscape, such as trees or fountains, are put on the stage, they are like an actor playing a role. In the example shown here, from the theatre at Chantilly, there are sets of landscape greenery on two sides of the stage, leading to a major fountain in the centre of the background. The audience sees landscape vegetation that consists of the painted sets mixed with living plants that have been brought on stage, while the fountain in the background of the stage is part of the permanent garden. The rear of the stage, in this case, opens onto the garden, which then becomes a 'real' background. But of course, this 'real' landscape is modified by being placed on the stage and by the painted landscape sets that lead up to it. Other examples can help to make the complex interplay among these elements clear and illustrate how they intensify and modify each other.

The painter, draughtsman, poet, dramatist and theatre designer Louis Carrogis

Salle à manger, the Hameau, Château de Chantilly, France, 2013. Photograph.
The interior of the salle à manger in one of seven rustic cottages commissioned by Louis Joseph, Prince of Condé, for his château in the 1770s. Joining pictorial traditions and landscape design, the salle à manger had plants and trees growing inside and its walls had painted forest scenes reversing the relation of interior and exterior.

(1717–1806; known as Carmontelle) put all of his skills to work in Parc Monceau, designed between 1773 and 1779 for the Duke of Chartres. In this case, he did not create a theatre in a garden, but rather a whole garden as a theatre, where one could travel through space and time. Describing it in his *Observations on Modern Gardening*, Thomas Whately wrote that 'movement animates the garden and makes the scenes of nature look like those of a dramatic representation'.[7] But the underlying concept of Parc Monceau was of a garden envisioned as a painting into which one could enter and move about.

In his *Essai sur les Jardins* (1774), Claude-Henri Watelet defined movement as the essential difference between a painting and a garden.[8] Movement could

also lead to 'theatrical scenes' since action was one of their key elements.[9] Historians have also pointed out the close connection between gardens and theatres in paintings of gardens, such as Antoine Watteau's 'La Perspective', which references Pierre Crozat's garden in Montmorency – a further example of the significant correlation between landscape and painting.

It was the cult of the 'natural', exemplified by Jean-Jacques Rousseau in *La Nouvelle Héloïse*, which brought an end to theatres in gardens and with it the demise of this complex form of representation in and of landscape.[10] Another aspect of this cultural shift was that people now sought from art the more complex picture that novels, by conveying what characters thought or felt rather than just what they did, could provide. These changes brought about a negative view of theatre and its ability to represent human activities. In Jane Austen's *Mansfield Park* (1814), the protagonist, Fanny, has a very low opinion of her cousins' decision to put on a play in their home.[11] Because addressing the role of time in landscape representation is an important issue for landscape architecture, it is particularly interesting to note that among Fanny's criticisms of the house theatre is the impossibility, within the timeframe of the play, of dealing with emotions like falling in love. As well there is the impossibility that all the action portrayed could have occurred in those few hours. As a result, in her view, the play made a mockery of the complexity of human feelings. Many French writers

A scene for *La fiera, el rayo y la piedra*, by Calderón, staged in Buen Retiro, Madrid, Spain in 1652. Engraving.
Highlighting the complex relationship between the illusion of theatre and the 'reality' of the stage, one of the wonders of Buen Retiro, a large palace complex built as a secondary residence in Madrid for Philip IV, was its Coliseo (1640). The Coliseo was a theatre that had an opening built into the back-stage wall that allowed the audience to view the palace's actual gardens.

were admirers of the English novel and similarly took up arms against theatrical productions.

The argument about whether theatrical representation is artificial or real in turn undermined the idea of theatrical representation in landscape. But it was not the first time that issue had been raised; such criticisms of the theatre had been voiced intermittently from the days of ancient Greece onwards, by Plato, by the French in the 18th century, and by Jane Austen and her contemporaries, among others. In the 20th century, these attacks gained new force, epitomised by art critic Michael Fried's statements that 'theater and theatricality are at war today with modern sensibility as such', and 'The success, even the survival, of the arts has come increasingly to depend on their ability to defeat theater.'[12]

The refined and subtle interplay between real and painted landscapes that existed in the 17th-century French garden still has, I believe, the potential to be part of both virtual and physical landscape projects in our own time. Some contemporary artists project images of landscapes onto real objects in the landscape – a highly interesting route to a new form for the rich landscape representation of the past.

Yet theatre as a part of a landscape is almost irrelevant today, except in the creation of public space. The modern open-air amphitheatre for gatherings in plazas and parks is an underused and impoverished remnant of the theatrical tradition in gardens.

Consisting mostly of a series of concrete steps, these amphitheatres are not intended to be artistic and do not connect with the art of representation. They are generic gathering places that do not serve any kind of gathering well; they have become a staid fixture of nominal public use, offering only tiers of seating and a hook-up to a power source for sound amplification.

However, there was a notable exception to this in the 1960s, when landscapes served as a gathering point for rock performances. One of the largest rock concerts of all time, the Woodstock Festival, was held outdoors on a farm in upstate New York. But the notion of establishing such communal gathering spots for enjoying the performing arts was subsumed soon after by the creation of monumental covered arenas that commercialised and interiorised the experience.

In addition, a related type of show takes place in landscapes today: the temporary staging of short-term events in parks. There are half a dozen such events each year in New York's Central Park, and they are typically held on the Great Lawn. Of course, that space was not designed for performances; it is flat. Therefore, during the events, the action on the covered stage is also shown on a huge screen set up on the lawn; without it, the audience would have a hard time seeing what is happening. As a result, what the public really sees is an electronically transmitted, enlarged visual image of the performers on stage. What they hear is an electronically magnified sound. So there is an absence of direct experience in this type of outdoor performance. What remains is the experience of being outside under the sky in a park on a summer or fall evening. It is the experience of landscape that is left.

This is not to say that there is an irreconcilable schism between the natural landscape and the digital age; there is the potential for interplay between electronic visual images and the landscape. At the Global Citizen Festival held in Central Park in late September 2012, for example, the background screen of the temporary stage reproduced the image of the stage and of the landscape in front of it, thereby extending the landscape to a greater depth. Through this device, the Great Lawn seemed a mile long – evoking one of the favourite tricks of landscape, and

certainly one that was used readily in 17th-century French gardens.

The question then is whether there are any modern artistic attempts to return the theatrical to the landscape. There are, but there are few of them. Among these are isolated but felicitous moments in Lawrence Halprin's work. His fountains are used as sets for performances, though (ironically) the cities that have commissioned the fountains are forever trying to stop, or at least contain, those performances. Halprin's fountains are not simply objects installed in a park or plaza, but significant landscapes themselves that elicit from visitors the desire to perform publicly, inspiring interaction.

The second example of representation of representation is one that does not involve theatre, but it does reflect the connection between painting and landscape.

Extending space as much as possible is important in landscape and can be accomplished virtually, visually or through representations in drawings. In the composition of landscape, it can be achieved by setting up a distant view or by making the frame or edge of a landscape disappear. There are also various examples of walls in urban gardens that were painted in a way that extended the garden virtually. It was a device to create the feeling of more space, a technique akin to that of the borrowed landscape in Japanese gardens.

Global Citizen Festival stage, Central Park, New York City, New York, USA, 2012. Photograph.
While most people were only able to see the Global Citizen Festival on large-scale monitors due to the flat ground-level where the performance was held, the event designers created a stage that appeared to extend the park view inside, creating the illusion that the park and stage were much deeper than in reality.

Salomon de Caus, Design for a trompe-l'oeil garden, 1612. Engraving with fold-out.
This diagram depicting a trompe-l'oeil garden is from chapter 25 of de Caus's *La Perspective avec la raison des ombres et miroirs* (London, 1612). With the treatise, de Caus, a French architect, garden designer, and hydraulic specialist, penned what is likely to have been the first theoretical discussion of the trompe-l'oeil garden.

(Overleaf) André Joly, *Le Château de Lunéville et le Rocher autour du bassin aux automates, c* 1742. Oil on canvas.
Uniting permanent theatrical performances, trompe-l'oeil painting, and landscape design, the King of Poland installed a massive rustic village with scenes brought to life by automata at the Château de Lunéville in the 1740s. Aside from the rustic vignettes, Lunéville's guests were able to admire painted perspectives hung behind three-dimensional grotto enclosures.

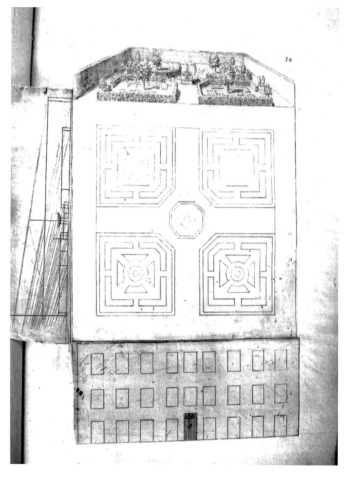

In the 17th and 18th centuries, French gardens made great use of this device. For instance, at the Château de Lunéville, while you may cringe at the literal style of the representation used in some wall paintings, they achieve their intended result. They extend the space significantly by deceiving the eye about the size of the garden and reaffirm the importance of the spatial dimension critical to landscape. The stories of some of these trompe l'oeils are provided in the captions, and sources for further reading are listed. But the examples are included here because they are capable of extending space.

The virtual dimension has become much more familiar with us today. For example, in the bar of The Modern restaurant at MoMA, where Thomas Demand's 2004 photograph of a very large landscape forest scene occupies one whole side of the space and makes it seem much deeper and longer than it is. The photograph is printed on glass, which adds to the feeling of looking outside through a window. But Demand's landscape work is interesting in another sense. His photographed landscapes are built by hand, leaf by leaf, trunk by trunk, branch by branch. This ties his work very neatly both to the theatrical tradition in landscape and to

trompe l'oeil. It extends the space, and it creates a faux landscape like those built in theatres.

Representation of Space: Depth and Width

Space needs to be represented in landscape renderings. This means representing something with three dimensions on a two-dimensional plane. (Landscape's fourth dimension, time, also needs to be represented on that plane; that issue will be discussed in the last section of this chapter.) Rules for painting that are well known to visual artists and designers were devised over time for precisely this purpose; beginning in the Renaissance, techniques for representing depth were developed.[13] One of the main issues involved was the relation of foreground to background and how they could be connected. This was achieved in part through the invention of the coulisse (avenue of trees) that focused the viewer's attention. That device was then used in actual landscapes as well. Over time, the middle ground became more and more important in joining the back and front planes, and the foreground became less and less significant, as one can see by comparing the frescoes of Masaccio (1401–1428) with the works of Piero della Francesca (1415–1492) and the large canvases by Veronese (1528–1588).

By the late 18th century, perhaps with John Constable (1776–1837), the sky – which until then had been only an awkwardly placed background – took on a life of its own and became an important part of

the composition. In JMW Turner's (1775–1851) work it came to nearly dominate the whole painting. The development of the representation of space over two centuries can thus perhaps be described as the process of the background advancing, coming to the fore, and finally taking over completely in Modernist paintings. That is now our visual reality.

In the past, the representation of depth in painting was carefully framed. The frame served the important role of separating the space that was represented from everything else around it, creating a world that you felt you could enter by way of the frame. This relates to the representation of the designed landscape and to the landscape itself in two interesting ways. First, there were ongoing efforts to find ways to use depth to go beyond the frame both in the actual, designed landscape itself and in its representation. You could say that the ha-ha (whose invention is credited by some to Charles Bridgeman and by others to William Kent) was intended to extend a designed site to include

Pietro and Ambrogio Lorenzetti, *The Effects of Good Government,* Palazzo Pubblico, Siena, Italy, 1338–39. Wall fresco.
On the walls of the Palazzo Pubblico in Siena, the frescoes of good and bad government use a wide format to convey a visual allegory for how to govern effectively over town and country.

John J Egan, *Panorama of the Monumental Grandeur of the Mississippi Valley,* **c 1850. Distemper on cotton muslin.**
In a monumental representation showcasing the expansive potential of landscape representation, an amateur naturalist commissioned the Irish artist John Eagan to paint a series of 25 panels some 106 metres (348 feet) in length with scenes from events on the Mississippi. Eagan's panorama was attached to two spools, which were to be scrolled while a 'delineator' narrated the scenes.

the landscape beyond it. It involves using a trench on the perimeter of a property to create the illusion that the landscape continues uninterrupted and remains unbound and unframed. As Horace Walpole observed, Kent also metaphorically 'leapt the fence and saw that all nature was a garden'.[14] The Japanese borrowed landscape was another technique, the aim of which was to transcend the frame of the landscape by leading your eye to a mountain, a tree or another element in the distance beyond the site. A contemporary example of this is the use of the ha-ha in Louis Kahn's Franklin D Roosevelt Four Freedoms Park, which eliminates the frame of the treed site's boundaries.

There are two indications that the actual breaking of the frame in the designed landscape had an effect on the way it was represented, resulting

in an attempt to undo the landscape frame in the representation of the landscape. The first is the use of the bird's-eye view, which usually includes quite a bit of context and many areas that are less defined as well as a fair amount of space that is left empty. In addition, the framing of a bird's-eye view is not the tight framing used in painting; the drawn image does not fill the space that abuts the edges of the frame.

The second way in which landscape transcends the frame and tries to capture space in its representation is not in depth but in horizontal extension, or width. The earliest examples of this are Chinese scrolls. They are of course paintings of real landscapes rather than depictions of landscape designs. They unroll in a long, narrow, horizontal format which transports you into different landscapes, including forests, mountains, small villages and house compounds. The eye travels along the scroll from one landscape to the next, focusing on a central scene but also seeing the changing landscapes on the periphery on either side of it.

Chinese scrolls contain the most extensive horizontality of all landscape representations. They differ considerably from Western traditions in their way of depicting the landscape. As Zijiang J He, a contemporary vision scientist at Louisville University, has pointed out, Chinese paintings rarely use a horizon line, and if they do, it is usually not visible. They also contain different scales; there is no front plane with large figures nor diminishing figures in receding planes

John Vanderlyn, *Panoramic View of the Palace and Gardens of Versailles,* **1818–19. Oil on canvas.** This panorama, painted by Vanderlyn, indicates a desire to capture spatial aspects of the landscape through width. Vanderlyn made sketches at Versailles years before creating the painting in New York. The expansive horizontal canvas was first installed in the Rotunda in lower Manhattan and later toured around America.

as you move back. As David Hockney shows in the video he made with Philip Haas, *A Day on the Grand Canal with the Emperor of China, or Surface Is Illusion But So Is Depth*, the changing scenes along the many miles of a riverfront, rendered in great detail on a 72-foot (23-metre) long 17th-century scroll, are landscape representations with multiple points of view; they are not based on the single-point perspective used in Western representation. As you travel down the river, you can see an entire village as well as the details of the interiors of shops and huts and of the activity on the streets in front of them; a whole villa and people reclining on the verandah; and towns, countryside, mountains, temples – an extensive, complex, inhabited world and landscape.[15]

In the Western tradition, the wide format is used in some Renaissance paintings that attempt to portray a city and its surrounding countryside, such as the Lorenzetti brothers' frescoes in the Palazzo Pubblico in Siena. But the format is much more dramatic in the panorama, which was extremely popular as a form of spectacle throughout the 18th and 19th centuries. It is a felicitous format for landscape, and it is not coincidental that sketchbooks with a horizontal layout are called landscape-format sketchbooks. Nor is it accidental that I requested that this book be designed in landscape format rather than in the vertical format used in architectural representation.

One of the most interesting extant examples of the panorama is a 106-metre (348-foot) long painting, *Panorama of the Monumental Grandeur of the Mississippi Valley*, which was commissioned by Dr Montroville Dickeson, an amateur archaeologist, and created by the Irish-American artist John J Egan around 1850. Egan's *Panorama* was exhibited in the 1850s, and Dickeson sometimes gave lectures about the scenes it depicted, which did not form a continuous image but instead consisted of 25 views of the Mississippi River at various points in history. The sweeping vistas of the river were a perfect match for the huge 19th-century panorama paintings. A contemporary of Egan's, John

Balmori Associates, Book of the Farmington Canal Greenway Masterplan, New Haven, Connecticut, prepared for the Town of Hamden, Connecticut, USA 1991. Brown ink drawing with photographs.
The 22.5-kilometre (14-mile) stretch of the linear park is represented in a 19.8-metre (65-foot) long, horizontal accordion-like form.

Fixed vs. handheld viewing devices
With a handheld device the experiment is about central vs. peripheral vision: the effect of field restriction. With a fixed device it's about sharing a particular view. In addition the function of the handheld device can be widely interpreted by the users as a hearing device or a megaphone for example.

Large
Height/lenght: 25"
S diameter: 2 1/2"
L diameter: 9 1/2"

Medium
Height/lenght: 13"
S diameter: 2 1/2"
L diameter: 5 1/4"

Small
Height/lenght: 13"
S diameter: 1 1/4"
L diameter: 5"

Paper
Height/lenght:12"
S diameter: 2"
L diameter: 5"

Balmori Associates, Faire des Ronds dans l'Eau / Making Circles in the Water, Métis Garden Festival, Métis, Canada, 2011. Digital rendering.
When progressing through the frames towards the water, focusing on the floating elements the field of view opens up, the horizon gets wider.

Balmori Associates, Faire des Ronds dans l'Eau / Making Circles in the Water, Métis Garden Festival, Métis, Canada, 2011. Digital diagram and photograph.
The viewing devices are truncated cones or tubes which vary in lengths and diameters and define the viewing field.

Rowson Smith, boasted that his panorama of the Mississippi would be four miles (6.4 kilometres) in length, 'one-third longer than any other pictorial work in existence'. It was, however, St Louis artist Henry Lewis who created the longest panorama actually realised, measuring three-quarters of a mile (1.2 kilometres).

Another example of a wide-format painting is John Vanderlyn's oval-shaped panoramic view of the palace and gardens of Versailles, which is now permanently installed at the Metropolitan Museum of Art. While Egan's painting was unrolled in front of viewers, Vanderlyn's massive work was meant to envelop them. Vanderlyn's panorama was originally displayed near City Hall in downtown Manhattan, in a specially constructed building, the Rotunda.

The panorama is such an appropriate format for landscape representation that my office used it when we had a long linear landscape to design for the 22.5-kilometre (14-mile) section of the proposed Farmington Canal Rail-to-Trail linear park described in Chapter 2. We created the masterplan as a panorama in which we incorporated hand drawings. It folded into a book format that was set up as a linear presentation around the walls of a conference room when we met with city officials and other stakeholders. This graphic format helped to convince the city of New Haven to fund the project.

The use of the panorama also leads to the consideration of perhaps the most fundamental concern in a designed landscape and its representation: the role of peripheral vision. As discussed in the previous chapter, in no other art is this issue so important. When my office was invited to design a landscape for the annual International Garden Festival in Métis, Canada, we chose a site looking out onto the St Lawrence River and channelled that view through a tunnel, creating the opportunity for people to experience the profound effect of limiting the field of view to central vision only, When you reached the end of the tunnel, you could also look at the landscape through tubes of varying dimensions that we installed.

Although modern artists are still under the sway of the persistent Picturesque view of landscape, they continue to struggle with the critical question of framing. When the artist Robert Irwin gave a lecture at Yale, he explained how he had moved away from painted or flat figures to 3-D pieces. In describing a framed painting on a wall, he said, 'I thought, well, let us remove that frame … but once you remove it, you realize that the frame is the wall on which the painting sits. If you go the next step, the frame is the room in which the wall is. To remove that you need to leave a space with walls and go into open space.'

Illustrated here are two present-day examples that deal with this issue. A surprising project by video artist Marina Zurkow breaks the convention of the edge of the frame by having a person, a bird or an animal walk into it from off stage, that is to say from

Marina Zurkow, Mesocosm,
Northumberland, England,
2011. Video still.
Zurkow describes Mesocosm
as 'an algorithmic work,
representing the passage of
time on the moors of Northeast
England. One hour of world
time elapses in each minute of
screen time, so that one year
lasts 146 hours.' In its escaping
the frame it introduces a
transformation of its space.

outside the assumed space. The other example, from
our office, expresses the desire to include the context
around the area we were designing to break the frame
of the picture and the assumed Picturesque setting
in order to introduce the modern city. At the same
time it is a critique of the frame and the separation it

creates from the surrounding context. Many design
interventions – even those that are relatively small –
become meaningless if they are not shown in their
larger context. In the real landscape, horizontal and
vertical interconnections with the surroundings (ie,
width and depth) are equally important. In landscape

Chapter 5 Historical Issues in Landscape Architecture Representation

representation, however, horizontal interconnections matter more. This in turn allows the panorama in its many iterations to take on a new meaning and importance for landscape representation.

The preferred elongated horizontal format – the landscape format – responds, I believe, to the real need to represent large spatial dimensions. There are many forms of landscape representation that attempt to do this, and in all of them you see the extension of vistas that is allowed by the landscape format. Landscape sketchbooks, the horizontal format of renderings for professional presentations, and the horizontal orientation of the screen for PowerPoint presentations are all clearly particularly well suited for conveying the width of a landscape.

Integrated Drawings

Since the connection between painting and landscape endures, if background is now the main subject in painting

and edges are questioned, does this have an effect on our representation of landscape today? I think that the frame is one of the reasons for my impatience and dissatisfaction with present forms of representation of designed landscapes. Yet some old forms of representation may help to point a way as we seek to 'break the frame' with what I will call 'integrated' representations that use a three-dimensional drawing

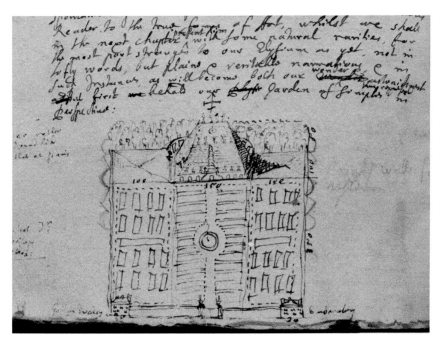

John Evelyn, Drawing in the manuscript of *Elysium Britannicum*, after 1659. Ink on paper.
In his *Elysium Britannicum, or The Royal Gardens*, Evelyn, a garden designer and author, produced the first monumental, encyclopedic work on 17th-century knowledge about horticulture. This manuscript shows a plan for a garden, seen from above, with a fountain, represented in perspective.

Anonymous plan for the Château de Dampierre, Dampierre-en-Yvelines, France, undated.
The landscape designer André Le Nôtre and the architect Jules Hardouin-Mansart built the French Baroque castle Dampierre for the duc de Chevreuse, between 1675 and 1683. A plan for the estate emphasises the seemingly vast size of the chateau in perspective, whereas the plane of the background is canted to stress the parterres and informal gardens that lie beyond it.

(for example, one using perspective) combined with a plan and/or a section together in one rendering.

In 1813 Thomas Hornor, decrying what he perceived to be the contemporary division between surveying and painting, wrote a text called *Description of an Improved Method of Delineating Estates*. In it, he described a drawing whose object 'is to combine the advantages of an exact plan with those of a landscape or perspective view'.[16] The virtue of this kind of drawing is that it opens the edges (the frame) and allows the landscape's surroundings to enter into the composition. In addition, it overcomes the abstraction of the plan and makes it become alive and more readable. It is nearly like building a model in front of the viewer, as some early and contemporary examples help to show.

In the complex hand-drawn rendering from the latter part of the 17th century shown here, a garden plan is integrated into the facade of a building. At the Château de Dampierre, a Le Nôtre garden and a Mansart building are integrated in a different fashion, by making a one-point perspective end in the layout of the plan above it. Barbara Stauffacher Solomon's coloured-pencil drawing of the agricultural flower fields in Lompoc, California, conflates a perspective plan and front view, but above all it reproduces the feeling that the fields evoke when you look at them from the highway. A model-like view with a perspective plan and section by Bernard Lassus gives a complete reading of the geometry of the site between the Pyramide du Louvre and the Arc de Triomphe in Paris. Our own conflation of a plan and perspectival view for a study of the landscape of a courthouse in Harrisburg, Pennsylvania, was done to overcome the flatness of the plan on a sloping ground. In a well-composed drawing, Dieter Kienast represents Garden M at Erlenbach through a superimposition of sections/elevations in two nearly

(Opposite) Barbara Stauffacher Solomon, LOMPOC, Santa Barbara, California, USA 1975. Coloured pencil on vellum. Stauffacher Solomon's drawings achieve a visual artistic integration of plan and perspective view, of landscape and architecture.

PERSPECTIVE AXIALE

Bernard Lassus, Proposal to reinvent Le Jardin des Tuileries, Paris, France, 1990. Ink on paper. Looking to the way that the new Louvre pyramid cut through its site to reveal its history, Lassus proposed to slice the Jardin des Tuileries to display its historic layers. The cross-section accompanying the perspective shows the proposed changes to the site. The integration of information is given separately in plan, section and perspective.

COUPE TRANSVERSALE
1:600

JARDIN DES TUILERIES

Bernard Lassus
Juillet 1990

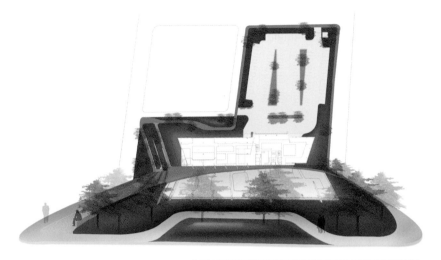

Balmori Associates,
Courthouse, Harrisburg,
Pennsylvania, USA, 2012.
Digital rendering.
This study of the landscape of a
Harrisburg courthouse conflates
perspective and plan.

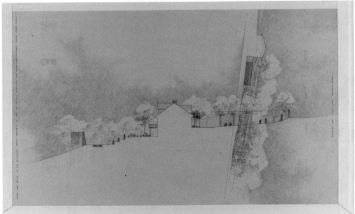

Dieter Kienast, Garden M
at Erlenbach, Switzerland,
1989. Grey and coloured
pencil on paper.
Section, elevation and
perspective are combined in
this drawing by Kienast.

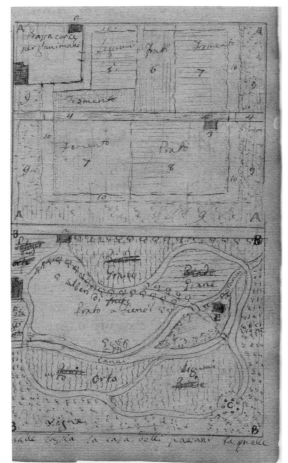

Francesco Bettini, Garden of M Donival (or Denival) before and after conversion, near Paris, France, mid-1770s. Ink on paper.
While living in France, Bettini commissioned his friend, M Donival (or Denival) to transform his garden of rectangular beds divided by a water channel into an irregular design. This early drawing of the extant site compares suggested interventions that might or might not be realised.

orthogonal cuts across the building and garden. Such integrated drawings were as rare in the past as they are now.

Representation of Time

It is curious that for a discipline in which everything is in constant change, there is so little in landscape representation that reflects time. The category of before/after renderings is perhaps the major exception. It is familiar to us through Humphry Repton's great depictions of an original property along with an attached overlay showing his intended interventions. (William Gilpin does something similar, but he uses two separate drawings, without Repton's clever montage.) However, there have been many other attempts to deal with this issue, using other approaches.

One of them is the sequential transformation of the same site, similar to the before/after representation. Another example of this, by Geoffrey Jellicoe, shows the transformation of a classical rose garden into a modern version. In another garden he designed, Jellicoe also undertook drawing the changes in the size of the trees every 10 years.

The issue of time in landscape has also been addressed by using drawing or photography to depict a site at two dramatically different times of day. This approach is used when evaluating a location and its characteristics. Photography – and above all, time-lapse photography – has captured this essential

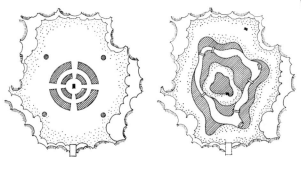

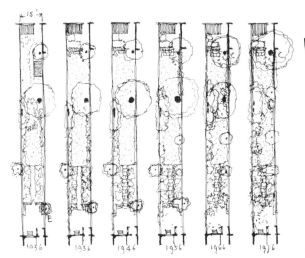

(Far left top) Geoffrey Jellicoe, The Rose Garden at Cliveden, Buckinghamshire, England, 1962. Marker on paper.
In 1962, Jellicoe redesigned the Rose Garden at Cliveden based on his view of Paul Klee's *The Fruit* (1932), which depicts an embryonic being inside of an apple. The drawings compare the existing formal garden to a looser design.

(Far left below) Geoffrey Jellicoe, Grove Terrace, Highgate, London, England, 1936–76. Marker on paper.
These series of garden plans show how the garden would grow over the course of five decades, to which Jellicoe commented, 'The mood of a garden can appear to have changed of its own accord, imposing its changes imperceptibly upon its owners.'

(Top left) Diana Balmori, *Early afternoon, Salisbury, England*, 1990. Coloured pencil on paper.

(Bottom left) Diana Balmori, *Late afternoon, Salisbury, England*, 1990. Coloured pencil on paper.
Showing the temporal effects of light on the landscape, these two coloured pencil sketches are of a site near where Constable loved to paint in the morning and afternoon.

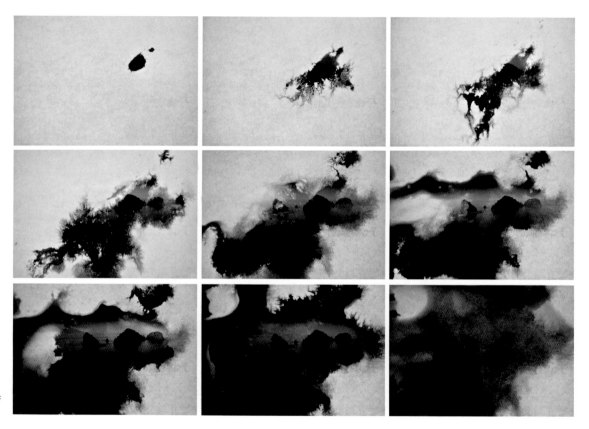

Mami Kosemura, *Frozen*, 2010. Paint on paper. Kosemura's work has been described as an accumulation of moments developed over time.

feature of landscape in other ways as well. That work has been done mainly by modern photographers and videographers, not landscape architects. Mami Kosemura's 2004 time-lapse piece, *Flowering Plants of the Four Seasons*, is even more complex. I first saw it as the final work in an exhibition titled 'East of

Eden: Gardens in Asian Art' at the Freer and Sackler Galleries at the Smithsonian in Washington, DC, and I was struck by the careful attention Kosemura paid to temporality. I have since collaborated with this Japanese artist and have incorporated some of her work in my lectures on the dimension of time. Her time-lapse projects involve more than photography. In *Under Water* (2007), rocks and water in a bay emerge from a dark black swirl and take form. They appear to be seen from the inside of a cave with water dripping from the ceiling – a landscape viewed through a waterfall. The images are worked over with brush and ink, sometimes on the film strip itself. Colours are introduced by hand. It is a hybrid, handcrafted, drawn image that is combined with a digital, photographic

one. This is where I think much of the new work with new digital images will take us.

The depiction of the different seasons has also been a way of capturing the essence of time. Bernard Lassus's Colas garden, as we have seen, takes the form of four sets of metal trees that are rotated through the year.

In an early project for the public space in the Winter Garden of the World Financial Center, on completion of the construction we put together an exhibition called 'This is not a Flower Show'. Its name played on the fact that an annual flower show would be held in the space soon after. The poster from the show illustrates the intention of depicting the eventual height of the palm trees (with white balloons), the palm

Bernard Lassus, Study of the winter planting beds with fake snow, Boulogne-Billancourt, France, 2001–2.

Bernard Lassus, Study of the summer planting beds, Boulogne-Billancourt, France, 2001–2. Photograph. Lassus looked to the idea of temporary landscapes in his Jardin du Jeu des Saisons. For the garden, Lassus made four sets of three different tree types in metal, each painted with a different seasonal colour scheme. The metal trees gave the garden's owners the possibility of playing with the seasons.

trees as very young plants, versus the ones installed, and a dead old palm tree lying among them. The intention was to cover the whole life cycle rather than to display the space with only the 15-year-old palms as a critique of the usual flower show with a plant at one moment only.

My office took still another approach to representing time for a project in China, capturing the way the landscape changed in the course of a day. It was a site with very sharp contours, so there was a dramatic contrast in the light and dark areas from morning to evening. And the change in water levels through the year was the important aspect of a project we did along a river in Iowa for a landscape that was designed to flood in sections. A much more sophisticated approach, which incorporates digital technology, is our study shown here of the Wave Garden in Beijing. Submitted for the 9th China International Garden Expo, the drawing gives time information over the course of 24 hours which itself was used to draw the landforms. It shows areas exposed to the sun over the day – information that was in turn used to make decisions about the plantings for the garden, now under construction.

Balmori Associates, *This is Not A Flower Show: An Installation on Cycles of Landscape (1989–1989)*, Winter Garden, Battery Park, New York City, New York, USA,1989. Perspectival digital rendering, printed on poster paper.
Poster for the exhibit.

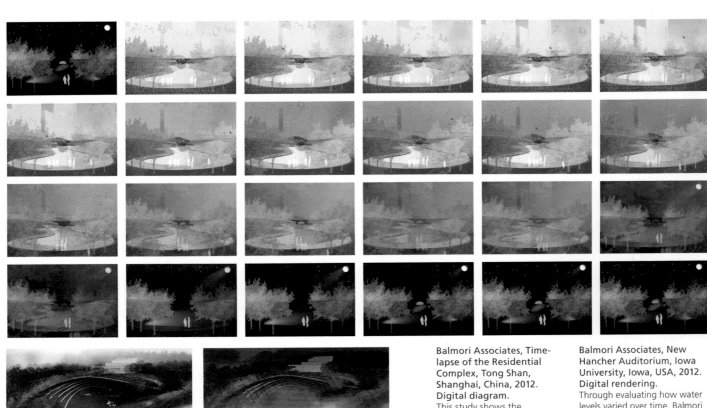

Balmori Associates, Time-lapse of the Residential Complex, Tong Shan, Shanghai, China, 2012. Digital diagram.
This study shows the differences in a site through its diurnal rhythm.

Balmori Associates, New Hancher Auditorium, Iowa University, Iowa, USA, 2012. Digital rendering.
Through evaluating how water levels varied over time, Balmori created a landscape purposely meant to flood in sections for this project. The rendering shows how the landscape is transformed by the rise of water.

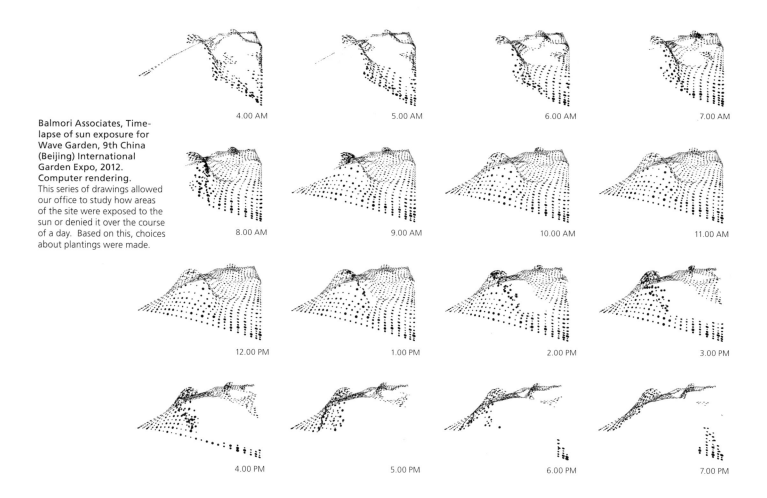

Balmori Associates, Time-lapse of sun exposure for Wave Garden, 9th China (Beijing) International Garden Expo, 2012. Computer rendering.
This series of drawings allowed our office to study how areas of the site were exposed to the sun or denied it over the course of a day. Based on this, choices about plantings were made.

4.00 AM

5.00 AM

6.00 AM

7.00 AM

8.00 AM

9.00 AM

10.00 AM

11.00 AM

12.00 PM

1.00 PM

2.00 PM

3.00 PM

4.00 PM

5.00 PM

6.00 PM

7.00 PM

References

1 William Chambers, *A Dissertation on Oriental Gardening* (London), 1772.
2 Quotation in Morris R Brownell, *Alexander Pope and the Arts of Georgian England*, Clarendon Press (Oxford), 1978, p 362.
3 Humphry Repton, *Humphry Repton: The Red Books for Brandsbury and Glemham Hall*, Dumbarton Oaks Research Library and Collection (Washington, DC), reprinted 1994.
4 F Hamilton Hazlehurst, *Jacques Boyceau and the French Formal Garden*, University of Georgia Press (Athens), 1966.
5 Christopher Hussey, *The Picturesque, Studies in a Point of View*, Routledge (London), 2004 [1927]. Gina Crandell, *Nature Pictorialized: 'The View' in Landscape History*, Johns Hopkins University Press (Baltimore), 1993, p 110.
6 Ibid.
7 Thomas Whately, *Observations on Modern Gardening*, T Payne (London), 1770.
8 Claude-Henri Watelet, *Essai sur les Jardins*, Prault (Paris), 1774.
9 Bram van Oostveldt, 'Ut pictura hortus/ut theatrum hortus: Theatricality and French Picturesque Garden Theory (1771–95)', in Caroline van Eck (ed), *Theatricality in Early Modern Art and Architecture*, Wiley-Blackwell (Malden, MA), 2011.
10 Jean-Jacques Rousseau, *Julie, ou la nouvelle Héloïse*, Marc-Michel Rey (Amsterdam), 1761.
11 Jane Austen, *Mansfield Park*, Thomas Egerton (London), 1814.
12 Michael Fried, *Art and Objecthood*, University of Chicago Press (Chicago), 1998, pp 163–8.
13 John White, *The Birth and Rebirth of Pictorial Space*, Faber and Faber (London), 1957.
14 Horace Walpole, *The History of the Modern Taste in Gardening*, Ursus (New York), 1995 [1771], p 43.
15 Philip Haas and David Hockney, *A Day on the Grand Canal with the Emperor of China*, Milestone Films (New York), 1991.
16 Thomas Hornor, *Description of an Improved Method of Delineating Estates*, J Harding (London), 1813.

6

Contemporary Issues Deriving from Change

The two subjects that are the most important to the immediate future of landscape representation have been brought about by constant change. On the one hand, the understanding of nature as something in constant change; on the other hand, the present acceleration of change due to human-related effects on the earth and its atmosphere. Related to both is the need to be able to work accordingly, accepting constant change, and to be able to represent it. Computing and hybridising of different data from different fields is at the forefront of creating a new language that can speak to constant change. But in the process, the fixed Arcadian images that have dominated the representation of landscape up to now need to be left behind. Computing can generate a new language, but this should not imply that its representation will be through computing only. These ideas serve as the coda to this book.

Computing and Hybridising

The concept of fields, networks and mosaics – a conceptual language derived from landscape history – is also the semiotics taken up by computing, bringing about the alignment of algorithmic language with landscape design. These ideas are in tune with our new understanding of nature as well as with the mechanisms of life, both of which are integral to landscape. This scheme was introduced by Christopher Alexander in his book *A Pattern Language* (1977), which claims to provide a complete working alternative to our present ideas about architecture and planning.[1] *The Timeless Way of Building*, the second volume of this three-volume series, has been adopted by interface and web designers, particularly on the West Coast, though it was written too early to address developments of the digital age.[2]

Finding ourselves woven into the constantly changing heterogeneity of nature, we can see it as a computing system that we can approximate with machines. I have used the word 'biocomputation' to describe the alignment of biological systems with landscape's aim to emulate them. Landscape designers are now concerned with how nature works, rather than with how it looks, as they were in the 19th century. Thus, landscape has abandoned its past efforts to mimic the external appearance of nature.

Computer code writing has blurred the line between the inanimate and the living – between technology and nature – and hybridised them. This algorithmic approach can include the mechanisms of life in a design or generate design based on how living systems function. In other words, computation can imitate many natural processes. Antoine Picon admires the algorithmic proponents' desire to emulate living processes in the design disciplines and calls it 'vitalistic'.[3] The hybridisation of the biological and digital worlds is one aspect of what is ahead; hybridisation is the most salient effect of the digital on the various disciplines.

In addition to bringing biology and landscape together through algorithms, computing has led to photography's hybridisation with digital media. Photography in landscape representation deserves a long separate treatment. It is another medium that some of us are interested in as a way of representing landscape, as is video, which offers valuable kinesthetic possibilities and is another topic that merits its own discussion. Photography today has been absorbed into the digital world of the design professions through Photoshop, the Adobe computer program created in 1995. As we are getting close to being able to draw directly by hand on computer screens, photography is combining with earlier media – such as drawing, painting and collaging – through computing, as is evident in the work of many contemporary photographers. Its hybridisation with painting was seen clearly in a recent show at the National Gallery in London which exhibited instances of the camera taking cues from painting, and vice versa.[4] Some cases left you guessing which of the two you were seeing. This is a rich field to mine for representation. Needless to say, most of the photography in the show was digital. The subject of the representation of space came up frequently, and the themes addressed seem very similar to those I have been considering in relation to landscape. For example, the photographer Sarah Jones commented in an interview: 'I am very interested in how space is articulated in the photograph. I am really interested in the way there is a sense of the subject being pushed right up towards you, that idea of everything almost sitting on the surface ... In many of my photos there's an appropriation of life-size, a one-to-one scale. The hanging height in the gallery recalls how the subject might have been originally experienced. And the width, how much you can get in your peripheral vision.'[5] It is important to note that the dominance of digital has brought about a new interest in analogue photography, which is immensely popular in photography programmes in art schools today, where darkrooms are quickly being reinstalled.

Chagrin over the current limitations of some computer programs, compared with the tools they replace, is tempered by the exciting new possibilities arising from biocomputation and hybridisation. Yet it is important to note again that today's digital world is flat; designers therefore have to produce patterns on a surface, which there are no software tools to enrich. Design programs such as Rhino interface badly with GIS programs, and GIS, in turn, makes it difficult to use cross-disciplinary information. Moa Carlsson, in her MIT Master of Science in Architecture (SMArchS) thesis, *Stratified, Destratified, and Hybrid GIS: Organizing a Cross-Disciplinary Territory for Design*, made a strong case for the greater inclusivity of cross-disciplinary information – as there is in McHarg's hand-drawn, stacked maps – and has stressed the significance of Dana Tomlin's statement that 'cartographic modeling [ie, modelling with thematic layers] is oriented more towards process than product'.[6] Carlsson's most critical point, however, is that McHarg's analogue GIS model 'provides not only a process for integration of cross-disciplinary data but also a representation of such, in the form of the composite map; ie, McHarg puts shape to the environment, available for manipulation in its totality.'[7] In other words she is stressing the *representation of the data*.

From a Fixed to a Changing Arcadia

Confronting the ever-changing aspect of nature presents landscape architecture with two new quandaries. First, the discipline is now in a contested territory, politically and culturally, since its new understanding of nature is not yet shared by society at large. A deep cultural divide exists between those who find the view of nature as constantly changing to be indispensable for engaging with the world, and those who resist this idea, hoping to remain in a static equilibrium, maintaining the status quo through technological fixes. In its iconic forms of representation, landscape attempts to show its public that the processes at work in it are under constant transformation, although that is not explicitly stated. The most immediate effect of this debate, however, is to put the discipline squarely in the middle of contemporary social and political issues.

The second quandary is the difficulty of representing constant change, particularly since the representation of landscape itself is so challenging. We have seen examples of attempts to deal modestly with change over time. However, the increasing pace of change means that we need to address this urgently. Periods of vigorous change, such as the present, provoke hybridisation and the convergence of fields – the creation of porous interfaces between disciplines. This blurs the distinction between subject and object. It is from these phenomena – convergence, emergence, hybridisation, interface, and continuity between subject and object – that new representation mechanisms will emerge. The reality of interface in particular has put an end to the illusion of any discipline being autonomous.

Constant and rapid change is affecting more than landscape. It is a general cultural phenomenon. The best example I can think of is Wikipedia, the crowd-sourced encyclopaedia of vocabulary and contemporary usage. Wikipedia also provides a history of changes. In looking up the concrete poet e e cummings today, I learned that the information about him had been updated 18 hours earlier and that the orthography I had always used in writing his name, with no capitalisation and no punctuation – the orthography he chose for his poetry – is no longer considered the correct way to write it. Instead, according to his estate, the preferred style is EE Cummings.

In the representation of landscape, one particular piece – the final rendering – plays a key role in the world of competitions through which most commissions are awarded today. This social document is an image of fixity; moreover, it is based on an ideal of permanence, intimating that landscape is eternal. The acceptance of change as a constant in nature has unravelled that implication, which is conveyed by the iconic rendering frozen in time; final renderings can no longer be viewed as images of an everlasting, paradisiacal landscape or Arcadia that speaks of an eternal equilibrium.

We are now in a new era. The Picturesque has been superseded, and landscape architecture must be reinvented. In Chapter 5, some examples of past representations of landscapes that dealt with changes over time are presented. However, their subtext was of an essentially immutable landscape, in which only a few specific elements, such as trees, ever changed.

In the 18th century, Hubert Robert and other designers, as well as engravers of landscape images, drew attention to ruins and to them being overtaken by the growth of vegetation, so both stressing the passage of time and consciously incorporating it into the designed landscape. Such images were also a reference to the fall of the powerful; the physical ruins of Classical buildings were symbols of the Roman Empire. It is not coincidental that Gibbon's famous book, *The Decline and Fall of the Roman Empire* (1776), was written in this same period.[8]

In the 17th century, representation of the actual landscape and theatrical pieces included not just buildings in ruins but dead trees and vegetation grown rampant, expressing the passage of a culture,

Dieter Kienast, Et in Arcadia ego, Private Garden of E on the Uetliberg mountain, Zurich, Switzerland, 1993. Photograph.
Kienast's sign 'Et in Arcadia ego' (I [death] am also in Arcadia) forms a boundary between the garden and the surrounding countryside.

of a time, and of a landscape. Claude Lorrain's 17th-century landscape paintings of Roman ruins are an early example of this.

In the English landscape designs of the 18th century, the ideal past took on a more complex set of references. The country estate architectural style was Classical, but in incorporating the Gothic in the form of separate garden pavilions or transitional pieces between the building and the landscape, landscape moved away from Classical composition.[9] These two temporal references, however, both harked back culturally to an Arcadia, classical or medieval, and expressed a yearning for a return to those golden ages. The classical Arcadia was a pastoral region of Ancient Greece regarded as a rural paradise – an idealised place or scene of simple pleasure. *Arcadia* later came to mean any vision of paradise: the biblical paradise of the Garden of Eden from which we were expelled; the medieval Christian paradise, exemplified by Dante's *Paradiso*; or the Renaissance vision of an earthly re-creation of the classical Arcadia.[10] Milton's *Paradise Lost* (1667) was the ultimate expression of this powerful cultural image. And when Alexander Pope was designing his garden at Twickenham, he too decried the loss of paradise:

Ian Hamilton Finlay with John Andrew Townsend, Monument to the First Battle of Little Sparta, Dunsyre, Scotland, 1984. Photograph. Hamilton Finlay has many references based on 'Et in Arcadia ego' adding modern forms of death to the inscription.

The Groves of Eden,
vanished now so long,
Live in description,
and look green in song.

For us, fixed Arcadias can be only of historical interest. We have left that world behind. In the early 20th century, painting, sculpture and architecture all made a dramatic break from it. In the 21st century, landscape is making that break as well, but with different results.

The embers of Arcadia glow through the ashes and reappear now in various guises, such as false paradises, that should be derided and eliminated. The present pursuit of the pleasure and repose that those places once offered, at least symbolically, is also scorned now. For instance, Ian Hamilton Finlay asserts that 'certain gardens are described as retreats when they are really attacks'.[11] However, this darker view of Arcadia is not entirely new. The most famous landscape image of all is Nicolas Poussin's painting of a pastoral Arcadia showing a tomb with the inscription 'Et in Arcadia ego' – 'I [death] am also in Arcadia' – so questioning the basic premise of a place without death, or without change.[12]

At the end of the rill in the private garden for E on the Uetliberg mountain in Zurich, Dieter Kienast has made prominent use of that inscription, though his biographer has clarified that this was at the client's request. But it attests to Arcadia's survival, if not for the designer, then for the owner of the garden. Kienast used 'Et in Arcadia ego' to signify 'end', leaving us to wonder whether it is the end of the garden (the inscription is placed on the property line), the end of the rill or the end of the idea itself.

The inscription also appears in Finlay's work in many guises – in prints, in poems, in plaques, and in engravings in stone in his garden 'Little Sparta'. As if to reinforce the idea presented in his aphorism of garden as attack and not repose, in Finlay's work 'Et in Arcadia ego' is always accompanied by images of contemporary weapons – tanks, machine guns and other modern symbols of death. The Arcadian image, therefore, survives as a reversal of its earlier assumptions or as a critique of them. At the same time, however, by using it we accept its power. It is this archetypal image that has been invoked by the final rendering in landscape presentations, sometimes unconsciously.

Instead of a landscape representation that strives to construct an image of paradisiacal fixedness, we are in need of poetic images that can capture change, images that say that they can and will change and yet still bring a state of joy. If anything is left of the Edenic garden, for us it is in discovering Arcadia in the fleeting moment, not in landscape images that recall a fixed, eternal paradise. As in the experience of the Japanese single-day celebration of cherry blossoms, whose petals flutter down in white showers as soon as the flowers have opened, our representations can contain the notion of passage and yet still bring us perfection and delight. The impermanence and brevity of a flower's life makes it beautiful. Beauty is in the poignancy of a life that scatters away.

References

1 Christopher Alexander, Sara Ishikawa, Murray Silverstein et al, *A Pattern Language: Towns, Buildings, Construction*, Oxford University Press (New York), 1977.
2 Christopher Alexander, *The Timeless Way of Building*, Oxford University Press (New York), 1979.
3 Antoine Picon, *Digital Culture in Architecture, An Introduction for the Design Professions,* Birkhäuser (Basel), 2010, p 100.
4 Hope Kingsley and Christopher Riopelle, *Seduced by Art: Photography Past and Present*, National Gallery, London, distributed by Yale University Press (New Haven), 2012.

5 Ibid, p 159.
6 Dana Tomlin, *GIS and Cartographic Modeling*, ESRI Press (Redlands), 2012, p 9; Moa Karolina Carlsson, *Stratified, Destratified, and Hybrid GIS: Organizing a Cross-Disciplinary Territory for Design* (MIT Master of Science in Architecture (SMArchS) thesis, June 2013), p 59.
7 Carlsson, ibid, p 105.
8 Edward Gibbon, *The History of the Decline and Fall of the Roman Empire* (Vol 1, 1776; Vols II–III, 1781; Vols IV–VI, 1788).
9 Diana Balmori, 'Architecture, Landscape, and the Intermediate

Structure: Eighteenth-Century Experiments in Mediation', *Journal of the Society of Architectural Historians*, Vol 50, Issue 1 (March 1991), pp 38–56.
10 A Bartlett Giamatti, *The Earthly Paradise and the Renaissance Epic*, Princeton University Press (Princeton, NJ), 1969.
11 Yves Abrioux, *Ian Hamilton Finlay; A Visual Primer*, Reaktion Books (London), 1985, p 38.
12 For a discussion of the interpretation of 'Et in Arcadia ego', see Erwin Panofsky, *Meaning in the Visual Arts*, University of Chicago Press (Chicago), 1955.

Project Team Credits

The projects are listed in the order in which they appear in the book.

High Line Park Competition, New York City, New York, USA: Balmori Associates, Zaha Hadid Architects, Skidmore, Owings & Merrill LLP, studioMDA

St Louis Waterfront, St Louis, Missouri, USA: Balmori Associates, HOK Planning Group, Greenberg Consultants, CDG Engineers, ABNA Engineering, Consulmar, Moffatt & Nichol, Vector Communications

Beale Street Landing, Memphis, Tennessee, USA: Balmori Associates, RTN Architects, Bounds & Gillespie Architects, Consulmar, L'Observatoire International

Godrej Masterplan, Mumbai, India: Balmori Associates, Pelli Clarke Pelli Architects, Atelier Ten

Farmington Canal Greenway, Extension at Yale University, New Haven, Connecticut, USA: Balmori Associates, Pelli Clarke Pelli Architects

American Revolution Center, Valley Forge, Lower Providence, Pennsylvania, USA: Balmori Associates, RAMSA

Shenzhen Cultural Park, Shenzhen, China: Balmori Associates, MAD architects

Wild & Us Competition, St Patrick Island, Calgary, Canada: Balmori Associates, Allied Works Architecture, David Skelly, NIPpaysage, Creative Concern, Knippers Helbig, Sherwood Design Engineers, Transsolar, Hanscomb, Anne Georg, Terry Bullick

Accrington Square, Lancashire, UK: Balmori Associates, s333, QUATRO, Larry Barth

Wave Garden, 9th China International Garden Expo, Beijing, China: Balmori Associates

Residential Complex, Tong Shan, Shanghai, China: Balmori Associates, Pelli Clarke Pelli Architects

Diana, Princess of Wales Memorial Fountain Competition, London, UK: Balmori Associates, Atelier Ten, Atelier One, Price & Myers, Long & Kentish, Grant Associates

Botanical Research Institute of Texas, Fort Worth, Texas, USA: Balmori Associates, H3 Hardy Collaboration Architecture

10 Li Park Competition, Public Administrative Town, South Korea: Balmori Associates, Joel Sanders Architect, MAD architects, EXE

The Bund Competition, Shanghai, China: Balmori Associates, Beyer Blinder Belle

VIOL Headquarters, São Paulo, Brazil: Balmori Associates, Pelli Clarke Pelli Architects

Masterplan for Public Administration City, Sejong, South Korea: Balmori Associates, HAEAHN Architecture, H Associates

Abandoibarra, Bilbao, Spain: Balmori Associates, Pelli Clarke Pelli Architects, Aguinaga y Asociados

Campa de los Ingleses Park, Bilbao, Spain: Balmori Associates, RTN Architects

Plaza Euskadi, Bilbao, Spain: Balmori Associates

Parque de La Luz, Las Palmas, Gran Canaria, Spain: Balmori Associates, Pelli Clarke Pelli Architects

Farmington Canal Greenway Masterplan, New Haven, Connecticut, USA: Balmori Associates

Faire des Ronds dans l'Eau / Making Circles in the Water, Métis Garden Festival, Métis, Quebec, Canada: Balmori Associates, Denis Pelli

Broadway Mall, New York City, New York, USA: Balmori Associates, Joel Sanders Architect

Courthouse, Harrisburg, Pennsylvania, USA: Balmori Associates, Ennead Architects

Winter Garden, Battery Park City, New York City, New York, USA: Balmori Associates, Pelli Clarke Pelli Architects

Iowa University Arts Campus Masterplan, Iowa City, Iowa, USA: Balmori Associates, Confluence

Bibliography

William Howard Adams, *The French Garden, 1500–1800*, George Braziller (New York), 1979

Roland Barthes, 'The Structuralist Activity (1963)', *Form* (1966), 12–14

Edmund Burke, *A Philosophical Enquiry into the Origin of Our Ideas of the Sublime and Beautiful*, 1757

Elizabeth Chirol, *Le Château de Gaillon*, M Lecerf (Rouen), 1952

Michel Conan (ed), *Contemporary Garden Aesthetics, Creations and Interpretations*, Dumbarton Oaks Research Library and Collection (Washington, DC), 2007

Michel Conan (ed), *Environmentalism in Landscape Architecture*, Dumbarton Oaks Research Library and Collection (Washington, DC), 2000

Michel Conan (ed), *Landscape Design and the Experience of Motion*, Dumbarton Oaks Research Library and Collection (Washington, DC), 2007

Michel Conan and John Dixon Hunt (eds), *Tradition and Innovation in French Garden Art*, University of Pennsylvania Press (Philadelphia), 2002

James Corner, 'Representation and Landscape', in Simon Swaffield (ed), *Theory in Landscape Architecture, A Reader*, University of Pennsylvania Press (Philadelphia), 2002, pp 144–64

Julia Czerniak, 'Challenging the Pictorial: Recent Landscape Practice', *Assemblage*, Vol 12, Issue 34 (December 1997), pp 110–20

Jean-Pierre Gabriel, *Erik Dhont: Jardins, paysages de l'invisible (Gardens, Hidden Landscapes)*, Ludion (Ghent-Amsterdam), 2001

William Gilpin, *Three Essays: On Picturesque Beauty; On Picturesque Travel; and On Sketching Landscape*, printed for R Blamire (London), 1792

Randy Gragg (ed), *Where the Revolution Began: Lawrence and Anna Halprin and the Reinvention of Public Space*, Spacemaker Press, 2009

Lawrence Halprin, *Lawrence Halprin: Notebooks*, MIT Press (Cambridge, MA), 1992

Lawrence Halprin, *Sketchbooks of Lawrence Halprin*, Process Architecture (Tokyo), 1981

John Dixon Hunt, *Nature Over Again: The Garden Art of Ian Hamilton Finlay*, Reaktion (London), 2008

John Dixon Hunt, 'The Question of the Picturesque', in *Fragments: Architecture and the Unfinished: Essays Presented to Robin Middleton,* Barry Bergdoll and Werner Oechslin (eds), Thames & Hudson (London), 2006, pp 267–74

Bernard Lassus, 'Obligation of Invention' in Simon Swaffield (ed), *Theory in Landscape Architecture, A Reader,* University of Pennsylvania Press (Philadelphia), 2002, pp 64–72

J Alden Mason, 'A Mississippi Panorama', *Minnesota History*, Vol 23, No 4 (December 1942), pp 349–54

Ad Reinhardt, 'Aesthetic Credo', *Poor.Old.Tired.Horse.* Issue 18

Humphry Repton, *Humphry Repton: The Red Books for Brandsbury and Glemham Hall*, Dumbarton Oaks Research Library and Collection (Washington, DC), reprinted 1994

Christian Tschumi, *Mirei Shigemori – Rebel in the Garden: Modern Japanese Landscape Architecture*, Birkhäuser (Boston and Basel), 2007

Index

Figures in italics refer to captions.

Picture Credits

The author and the publisher gratefully acknowledge the people who gave their permission to reproduce material in this book. While every effort has been made to contact copyright holders for their permission to reprint material, the publishers would be grateful to hear from any copyright holder who is not acknowledged here and will undertake to rectify any errors or omissions in future editions.

Front and back cover drawings © Balmori Associates/ Angela Chen-Mai Soong and Noemie Lafaurie-Debany

pp 15, 33, 35, 49, 50, 51, 52, 53, 54, 55, 56, 77, 110 (l), 115, 141 (r), 153, 156, 174 (tr & br), © Diana Balmori; p 22 The Architectural Archives, University of Pennsylvania; p 24 Image courtesy of the Mississippi River Commission; p 26 © Balmori Associates/yi-Feng Lin; p 27 © Balmori Associates/Kyle O'Connor; p 28 © Balmori Associates/Julia Siedle; p 29 © Christopher Rauschenberg; p 36 © David Hockney; p 38 © Balmori Associates/Alice Feng; p 43 © Peter Shepheard Collection, Library and Archives of the Landscape Institute; p 44 © The Trustees of the British Museum: Department: Prints & Drawings: Registration number: 1964,1104.1.6; pp 45 (l) , 108, 109, 110 (r), 111, 112, 113, Lawrence Halprin Collection, The Architectural Archives, University of Pennsylvania; p 46 © Elizabeth Mead; p 47 © Kenneth Helphand; p 48 © Laurie Olin; pp 57, 58 © Martha Schwartz Partners; pp 59, 60 © Kongjian Yu/Turenscape; p 61